$\mathcal{S}$OTHEBY'S

GUIDE TO

ORIENTAL

CARPETS

BY WALTER B. DENNY
ILLUSTRATIONS BY NORMA JEAN JOURDENAIS

A FIRESIDE BOOK

Published by Simon & Schuster

New York   London   Toronto   Sydney   Tokyo   Singapore

FIRESIDE
Rockefeller Center
1230 Avenue of the Americas
New York, New York 10020

Copyright © 1994 by Sotheby's Inc.

Cover art: Lisan Türkmen Main Carpet, West Central Asia, 19th century. Detail.
15'16″ × 7'10″. Courtesy of Sotheby's.

Sotheby's Books
New York • London
Director: Ronald Varney
Executive Editor: Signe Warner Watson
Associate: Allegra Costa
Specialist: Mary Jo Otsea, Vice President, Rugs and Carpets

Manufactured in the United States of America
10 9 8 7 6 5 4 3 2 1

Library of Congress Cataloging-in-Publication Data
Denny, Walter B.
    Sotheby's guide to oriental carpets / by Walter B. Denny; illustrations by
Norma Jean Jourdenais.
        p.   cm.
    "A Fireside book."
    Includes bibliographical references and index.
    1. Rugs, Oriental—Collectors and collecting.   2. Rugs, Islamic—Collectors
and collecting.   I. Jourdenais, Norma Jean.   II. Sotheby's (Firm)   III. Title.
NK2808.D39   1994
746.7'5'095075—dc20   94-30270
                                                                          CIP

ISBN 0-671-89946-5

For Uncle Charlie

CONTENTS

SOTHEBY'S

GUIDE TO

ORIENTAL

CARPETS

CHAPTER 1

HY
COLLECT
ORIENTAL
CARPETS?

An Introduction

If one were to conjure up an imaginary dinner party with a guest list consisting of Cardinal Wolsey (prime minister to King Henry VIII of England), Charles Martin Hall (the discoverer of the process of refining aluminum), Erich Maria Remarque (author of the great World War I novel *All Quiet on the Western Front*), the painter Henri Matisse, and Kareem Abdul-Jabbar of the Los Angeles Lakers, what would be the topic of conversation? Since all of these individuals are, or were, collectors of Oriental carpets, it is highly likely that a spirited discussion over the meal would focus on the trials, tribulations, and triumphs of collecting.

As our guest list suggests, carpet collecting has been around for a long time. The earliest carpets from the Middle East to have survived in any significant quantity—those made in Turkey in the fourteenth century—were not only collected but even copied in Western Europe. By the fifteenth century, carpets from the Islamic world of the Middle East were familiar to most Europeans of the land-holding and merchant classes, both because of their importation in large quantities and because of their depiction by European painters. In fact, many of the reasons that play a part in collecting carpets today have been around for 700 years, and collecting as a sustained phenomenon in the history of European taste has continued—with few interruptions—for well over half a millennium, making it one of the oldest forms of art collecting practiced today.

Why carpets? Why has this art form, deeply embedded in the history, societies, and cultures of the Islamic lands of the Middle East, become so fascinating to collectors in lands and cultures remote from the natural habitat of the Oriental carpet? What is the secret of the fascination that carpets have elicited from Western collectors for such a long time? To aid us in answering these questions, we have an interesting body of evidence surviving in European written documents about carpets, and in the hundreds upon hundreds of European paintings created over the centuries that depict Oriental carpets as they were collected in Europe and later in North America.

POWER, PRESTIGE, WEALTH, AND HOLINESS

To begin with, we should note that available early documents point out one feature of Oriental carpets that has changed little over time: Good examples are sometimes expensive, and they are often hard to find. From the fourteenth century onward, the journey from the Middle East to European markets, whether by sea or by land, was fraught with hazards, from the recurring sea and land warfare between the Ottoman Turkish Empire and its European enemies, to the dangers of storms, shipwrecks, pirates, and brigands. A high demand in Europe for these colorful woven treasures of the East ensured a brisk commerce in carpets, and subjected carpets, then as now, to high rates of duty at ports of entry and border crossings, keeping prices high. These high prices, in turn, often made the owning and displaying of carpets an indication of good taste, wealth, and power. So to begin with, carpets were costly items, and the cost alone contributed in part to their mystique. But cost and monetary value alone are only a small part of their appeal to Western collectors, and many of the greatest carpet collections of recent years have been accumulated by individuals whose taste, energy, and knowledge more than amply compensated for their modest financial resources.

Another aspect of carpets that more subtly affected the history of collecting was their association with religion. For centuries, if not for millennia, textiles have been associated with sanctity and holiness. The veil of Solomon's temple mentioned in the Bible is the predecessor of today's *parokhet,* or Torah curtain, that covers the Scriptures in a synagogue. The table of the Lord's Supper, with its attendant table linen, became the altar of the Christian church. As a deference to holiness or to royalty, laying one's cloak on the ground under the feet of a prophet or sovereign represented an ultimate gesture of reverence, as the stories of Palm Sunday or Sir Walter Raleigh's famous gesture to Queen Elizabeth amply demonstrate. In the Islamic world, mats or carpets covered the floor of a community prayer hall or mosque, providing the canonical "clean" place for worship required for Muslims.

All of these associations between textiles and reverence formed a part of the general consciousness of carpets in Europe over 600 years ago, and little had changed by the 1950s, when an American broadloom manufacturer's slogan was "A title on the door needs a Bigelow on the floor." In practical and symbolic custom, costly Oriental carpets were placed on the floors in front of cathedral altars and became a standard part of the ritual furnishings of the Roman Catholic church. When a bishop or pope died, the body was laid out on an Oriental carpet at the funeral. When a king, nobleman, or merchant had his portrait painted to preserve his image for posterity, an Oriental carpet was shown under the royal feet, or on top of a table next to the seated noble subject.

Most significant of all, perhaps, was the depiction of Oriental carpets under the feet of saints or of the Virgin Mary. This embellishment was again given a permanent niche in the history of European taste because of the many important altarpieces—the most publicly visible and frequently looked-at paintings created in the fourteenth through the sixteenth centuries—where

11

artists have clearly depicted Oriental carpets under the feet of the Mother of Christ herself (Plate 17). Van Eyck, Memling, Bellini, Mantegna, and a host of other European painters have enshrined the popular image of the Oriental carpet's associations with sanctity and piety, another important reason for the popularity of carpets with European collectors.

If we were to look at the phenomenon of carpet collecting solely as a reflection of pride in wealth, an association with sanctity, and an amalgam of vanity, covetousness, and pride, we would however be ignoring the most important reason for the sustained history of carpet collecting over the centuries—and the reason why it has continued when other types of collecting have gone in and out of fashion. For, in addition to their utilitarian and symbolic functions, many carpets are also magnificent works of art. While they have not always been appreciated as such, especially in times that valued art only when it bore a signature, title, or place-name, the powerful visual appeal of beautiful carpets has always found appreciative response among collectors. In fact, carpets constitute one of the most distinctive and important cultural and artistic achievements of Islamic civilization. Their ability to give their owners pleasure through their qualities of design, texture, color, meaning, and traditional functions has shown over the centuries a truly remarkable tendency to transcend borders of religion, culture, and politics. Carpets were made on all levels of the traditional societies from which they came, from the humblest village cottage or nomad's tent to sophisticated commercial manufactories and court design ateliers. And through much of the history of Western taste since 1300, they have appealed to a wide collecting public, from kings and courtiers to middle-class merchants; in our own time, their following is even wider. With the possible exception of silk textiles and Chinese porcelain, no other artistic medium has shown this ability to transcend cultural and social borders. To get an idea of the artistic reasons for this phenomenon, let's begin with a defnition of the Oriental carpet itself, and with an examination of how carpets were created in the lands of their origins.

A LONG AND
COLORFUL HISTORY
IN EAST AND WEST

The history of carpet collecting in the European and Western world goes back many centuries, and is recorded in many ways. Wills and probate records, descriptions of royal gifts, inventories of the treasures of great houses, and the registers kept by customs posts on international borders all help to give us a picture of the movement of carpets from east to west, from at least as early as the fourteenth century C.E. (In this book, we use the neutral indication C.E.—"of the common era"—in preference to the religious term A.D.) But, as we have mentioned, much of what we know about the early history of carpets comes to us from an unexpected source: the hundreds upon hundreds of securely datable paintings—altarpieces, genre scenes, portraits, still lifes, and historical paintings—in which European artists depicted these colorful treasures with great accuracy. The very earliest carpets from the Middle East to have survived in intact form into our own time date from the fourteenth century, and it is likewise from the fourteenth century that European artists first begin to depict Oriental carpets in their paintings. Carpets from Turkey arrived via Mediterranean sea routes into Italy, especially into the great port of Venice, and were depicted by painters from Florence and Siena. Here they graced the houses of great merchant and banking notables, and were used in the urban churches whose wealth came from the protection and patronage of noble families.

By the fifteenth century, Oriental carpets were more or less a commonplace type of interior furnishing in well-to-do homes in Italy and, to a similar extent, in Flanders and France. Small carpets, strikingly similar to those woven in the nineteenth and twentieth centuries, appear in numerous depictions of middle-class interiors; the cloth merchant Arnolfini and his wife, immortalized in Jan van Eyck's famous wedding portrait of 1434, owned a small Turkish rug that they kept beside their bed. In Venice it was customary to hang carpets out the windows on feast days, and when the Senate and doge paraded through St.

Mark's Square, hundreds of Oriental carpets decorated the balconies and loggias of the surrounding buildings. At the end of the fifteenth century, carpets flooded into Europe by land and by sea; the surviving records from around 1500 of a customs post on the frontier between Transylvania and Hungary show several hundred "Turkish carpets" passing north in an eight-month period.

Since the owning of an Oriental carpet was then as now a sign of intelligence and good taste, it was natural that when one sat for a portrait, a carpet was included in one's surroundings. In these early times, carpets were rarely depicted on the floor, except under the feet of kings or saints. Rather, they were placed on tables, where they were protected from dirt and damp, and could be seen and touched to best advantage. From the many portraits from throughout the sixteenth century, and from the still lifes and genre scenes that began to emerge toward the beginning of the seventeenth, come hundreds of depictions of carpets that allow us not only to date individual design types, but give us a record of their rise and fall in popularity among European collectors. From the paintings of this time stems the practice among carpet historians of using the names of painters to categorize groups of carpets: Holbeins and Lottos, Memlings, Crivellis, and Bellinis are well-known designs that bear witness to the role that European painting plays in understanding the history of Oriental carpets.

By the seventeenth century, the depictions of carpets gradually began to wane in the painting of Italy and France, as these countries developed a new unified concept of style in interior decorating. By contrast, in the rich middle-class cities of Holland, depiction of carpets reached a new height in the works of Dutch painters, and the Dutch collector was exposed in the marketplace to a multitude of carpets from Iran and India, as well as the familiar examples from the Ottoman Turkish realms. A curious effect of the Reformation on carpet collecting was the use of Oriental carpets (whose designs had no religious or symbolic meaning for Europeans) as decoration in Protestant churches, where John Calvin had forbade the use of religious paintings, stained glass, and statuary. Gifts of carpets to the local churches from local notables in the seventeenth and eighteenth centuries attested to the vigorous pace of collecting, especially in central and south-central Europe.

By the latter part of the eighteenth century, especially after the rise of neoclassicism in European art, the collecting of Oriental carpets diminished among that element of the European aristocracy that followed French style and manners, to be replaced by carpets named Wilton and Savonnerie, Gobelins and Aubusson. At the same time, political calamity in Iran and economic collapse in Turkey led to a diminishing quantity of rugs woven in the Middle East for export to Europe. But in the nineteenth century, collecting began anew, partially as a result of European colonial expansion in the Islamic world, and partially as a result of the romantic revolution in taste that allowed many styles to exist side by side. By the late nineteenth century, the founding of the great European museums of decorative arts—in London, Paris, Budapest, and Vienna—saw the first interest of art museums in acquiring examples of carpets from the Middle East. Meanwhile, the first books on carpet collecting began to appear in various European languages, and collectors ranging from the creators of great industrial, mercantile, and financial fortunes to middle-class merchants and professionals turned once again to the Oriental carpet as a focus of collecting.

It is in the twentieth century, however, that the greatest explosion of interest in the Oriental carpet has occurred. The first collector organization, the New York Hajji Baba Club, was founded in the 1930s; by the late fifties, the first important exhibition of nineteenth-century village and nomadic weaving was mounted at the gallery of the Asia Society in New York. The American collectors James Ballard and Joseph McMullan formed collections of carpets that were not limited to the great "classical" examples of the fifteenth through the seventeenth centuries, but included examples from the eighteenth and nineteenth centuries as well, and they valued these later examples as works of art fully equal to their older forebears. The donation of these two great collections to American museums, and similar gifts in the United States and elsewhere, brought into museum collections examples of village and tribal carpets. These tended to replace the earlier carpets woven for court and commerce, and increasingly formed the focus of interest of farsighted collectors. By the late 1960s, the number of collectors exploded; this in turn fueled the publication of hundreds of books, the mounting of dozens of exhibitions, and the emergence of new collector organizations and magazines devoted to the interests of carpet collectors. Today there are collector clubs everywhere from New York to New South Wales, and at periodic international conferences on Oriental carpets, collectors from Brisbane and Boston, Paris and Pittsburgh, flock to hear papers on subjects both general and arcane. Collectors of Kashan carpets and Kazak carpets can find many others who share their specific obsessions, and there is a general exchange of information as well as of carpets themselves.

The primary uniting bond among the contemporary collectors of carpets is a shared appreciation of the beauty of the art form. While there are those who have been tempted to collect because of the investment potential or social cachet, today's collecting is above all fueled by a passionate response to the textures, colors, patterns, layouts, and motifs of carpets—as well as by the considerable ambiguity and mystery that still surround many of their designs. This heady mixture of aesthetic and intellectual interest, sometimes as bewildering to the outsider as it is intoxicating to the collector, is still nowhere near as mysterious as it sometimes appears to be. In this introductory book, our primary task will be to show how the world of carpets is one where a good eye for beauty and a good head for common sense can bring the novice collector a great deal of confidence and satisfaction, and where the pathway to increased knowledge is full of excitement and beauty.

CHAPTER 2

HAT IS A CARPET?

THE GEOGRAPHY AND CULTURE OF CARPETS

Broadly defined, what we call a *rug* in these pages is a heavy textile made for a wide variety of utilitarian, symbolic, or aesthetic purposes, usually destined to be used essentially in the form in which it leaves the loom, without cutting or tailoring. What we call a *carpet* is the most important subclass of rugs, usually rectangular in shape and meant to be used on a flat surface such as a floor, wall, or tabletop. Generally speaking, the terms *Oriental rug* or *Oriental carpet*, which most of the time will be used interchangeably in this book, refer to objects made in what we today call the Islamic world, from Morocco in the west to central Asia

17

in the east. It is a cultural environment defined in large part by the dominant Islamic religion and its associated peoples and their customs, and in a geographical zone sometimes defined as the "rug belt." Oriental rugs were and are also made by non-Islamic peoples in places like China, and by non-Muslim minority weavers throughout the Islamic world. In addition, today and in the past, economic factors have led to the production of rugs using traditional Oriental designs and woven in traditional Oriental techniques in places as diverse as England, Spain, Romania, and Hong Kong.

What is this "rug belt," the traditional homeland of Oriental rugs and carpets? In our map, the shaded lands where rugs were and are traditionally woven share many traits in common in addition to their prevailing Islamic religion and culture. For one thing, they consist, environmentally speaking, of large amounts of marginal land unsuited either for intensive agriculture or for intensive habitation, because of poor soil, limited rainfall, mountainous terrain, or sparse vegetation. But what is a poor environment for farmers, villagers, and city dwellers constitutes the traditional homeland of herders of sheep and goats. These animals, which in large numbers are destructive of vegetation of all kinds, from grass to trees, are banned from rich farming areas but thrive in the semiarid uplands and mountain pastures of the Islamic world. The nomadic or seminomadic peoples who tend these animals, and who market their milk, flesh, hides, and fleece, formerly constituted major elements of society in the traditional Islamic world. From the uplands of Morocco, Algeria, and Tunisia to the semiarid deserts of Arabia, northern Iraq, and Syria, to the mountainous terrain of the southeastern Balkans, Anatolian Turkey, Transcaucasia, Iran, and Afghanistan, to the flat sandy wastes of what are now the new Islamic central Asian republics, nomadic peoples have for many centuries herded the animals whose hair and wool traditionally constituted the major source of fiber from which Oriental carpets are woven. In addition to arid climate and sparse vegetation, these traditional lands of the rug belt generally show one other characteristic: a variable climate with sufficient periods of cool or cold weather. The extreme temperatures served as a further impetus for the use of

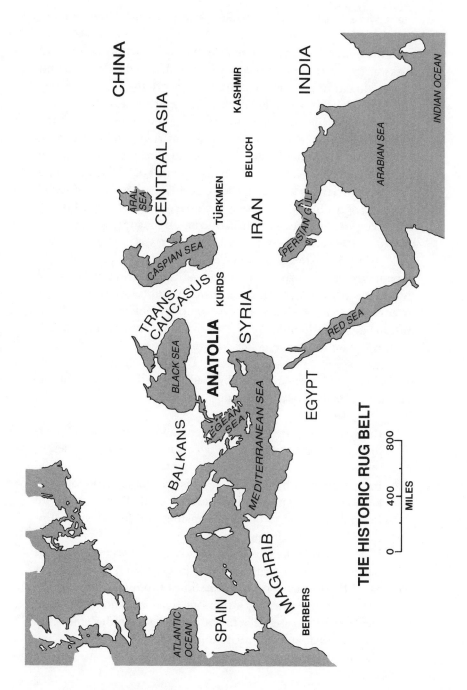

THE HISTORIC RUG BELT

0   400   800
|____|____|
MILES

heavy wool textiles to insulate against the cold in the traditional dwelling place.

In the nomadic encampment or in the village whose communal flocks graze on the hillsides away from cultivated fields, we find rug-making at its most elemental level, close to the source of fibers that make up the traditional carpet. There are several theories as to where the carpet and its techniques originated historically; the leading view among scholars today is that rugs originated as an art form among nomadic and seminomadic peoples who lived in tents and villages, and subsequently permeated Islamic urban and court society. The reasons for this diffusion across the social spectrum of traditional society may in part be found in the history of the rug belt, where established urban dynasties, with sophisticated economies and court establishments, were time after time replaced by dynasties of nomadic or rural tribal conqueors. These outside groups in turn settled into traditional urban patterns of living, while bringing with them customs and tastes of the village or encampment. Such artistic cross-enrichment thus provided a multilevel social habitat for the traditional Oriental rug, which we can divide for convenience into four layers.

These layers, first set out by the German scholar Kurt Erdmann in the 1950s and restated by the British scholar Jon Thompson in the 1980s, are as follows:

1. Rugs woven in traditional designs and for traditional uses, primarily for the use of the weavers and their families in the traditional weaving environment.

2. Rugs woven in traditional designs and for traditional uses, both for local consumption and as a kind of "cash crop" to be traded or sold to obtain necessities and luxuries not produced in the traditional environment.

3. Rugs woven in a variety of traditional and market-conscious designs, often in nontraditional formats, and primarily for sale. These carpets were sometimes produced through the cottage industry or putting-out system, and sometimes through urban manufactories usually under the control of businessmen entrepreneurs and, more recently, of weaving cooperatives.

4. Rugs woven in special workshops either belonging to royal courts or under court control, and using special, often one-of-a-kind designs and styles created by professional court artists. Such carpets were usually meant either to be used in the palaces of royalty and nobles or for royal gifts and ceremonies.

These four layers of rug production, then, demonstrate that rugs were originally woven by and for people in all social and economic classes in their traditional societies. The many origins and many intended uses of Oriental rugs together constitute one of the major reasons why these rugs became so popular in non-Oriental societies, and why the designs and techniques of the particular Oriental rugs were copied and imitated in many places in the Orient and the Occident.

The pervasive urban and Western conception of an Oriental rug or carpet in our time is as an attractive form of floor covering, a form of interior decoration. This is, of course, a major use of rugs in their original habitat, but only represents one kind of use for which rugs were woven. In the nomadic encampment, where the rug form may have originated many centuries ago, rugs do function as floor covering in the fabric tent or domical *yurt*, a dwelling made of poles lashed together and covered with fitted slabs of felt (Illus. 1). But rugs also serve as parts of the dwelling itself: Tent bands, rugs up to twenty meters in length, hold the felt covering on the yurt, and a type of rug known as an *ensi* may serve as the actual roll-up door for the dwelling. In the interior, rugs made into bags of various sizes hang on the walls, serving as containers for clothing, utensils, tent stakes, grain, flour, and wool; other bags are used to store quilts, bedding, and other rugs. Smaller rugs are fashioned as handbags, saddlebags, and brief-cases to carry valuables and money. Yet other bags may hold baked bread, or cushion pottery vessels. And for rites of passage such as weddings and circumcisions, or for other tribal celebrations of a religious nature, special rugs were often woven as colorful trappings for animals. These served as examples of a bride's artistic accomplishment in her dowry, and as demonstrations of a family's wealth and weaving skills.

This rich variety of rug functions and genres, found at the most elemental level of rug production, is almost always the artistic product of women. In tribal and village rug production, with very few exceptions, rug-weaving is the exclusive activity of girls and women. Designs and techniques peculiar to the tribal group or village are traditionally passed down from generation to generation—from mother to daughter and from sister to sister—as young women learn weaving as an essential part of their social and economic roles. Together with other traditional weaving arts, no other art form demonstrates this degree of social embeddedness as well as social pervasiveness, both factors that led to a remarkable degree of artistic and symbolic continuity in rugs as they have evolved as an art form over the centuries.

1. Traditional yurt nomadic dwelling, central Asia

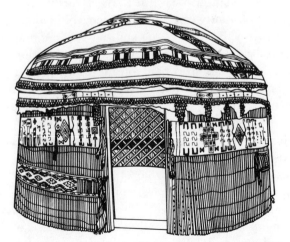

THE TECHNIQUE
AND MANUFACTURE
OF CARPETS

One of the most daunting features of rug books for the novice is the often mysterious and arcane section dealing with the technique and structure of carpets. In fact, if we look generally at textiles, the techniques used to make Oriental rugs are very simple. An American tourist sitting down at a loom in Rabat or Kayseri can learn the basic technique of knotting a carpet in a matter of minutes, and despite the impression sometimes conveyed by the diagrams found in rug books, the various subtypes of carpet knotting are not only easy to make, but usually easy to identify in the final product. The problem for the novice arises from trying to envisage a soft, three-dimensional object woven from fiber as it is depicted by an artist on a two-dimensional page. Our drawings have been carefully made to be as helpful as possible, but if they prove perplexing, a brief encounter with a rug itself in the company of a competent guide will usually make everything clear.

A. MATERIALS
Most Oriental rugs are made either completely or primarily of wool. The wool of sheep is the most miraculous of fibers; it is strong, soft, resistant to sunlight and rot, is easy to spin into yarns, and is easily dyed in beautiful colors; it sheds wrinkles quickly and is supple and elastic when spun. Goat hair is usually less easy to spin and dye than wool, but is sometimes used in certain locales for the warp and weft, the muscle and sinew, that form the foundation of a rug. Cotton, the best-behaved of natural fibers, is sometimes also used for the foundation of a rug, but is rarely incorporated into the visible part of a rug's structure.

Liberating the woolly fleece from its host is not easy; sheep often react to haircuts in the same manner as three-year-old children, but sheep are both heavier and stronger. In traditional

2. Traditional scissors used in sheep-shearing

societies of the Middle East, hand shears forged of a single piece of steel (Illus. 2) are used to clip the squirming, bleating sheep. The fleece, once separated from the sheep, has nothing to do with the white-as-snow image of Mary's Little Lamb. It is extremely oily (*lanolin* literally means "oil of wool")—and usually both very dirty and inhabited by hordes of squatters with six or eight legs. The cut fleece must be washed (*scoured* is the term we sometimes quite appropriately use) and then combed with special tools (*carded* is the technical term) to render it clean and fluffy and ready for spinning (Illus. 3). In the process of spinning, a clump of carded wool is held in the left hand; a small bit of wool is pulled from the clump and attached to a small hook or slot in a device known as a *spindle* (Illus. 4), that closely resembles an old-fashioned toy top. The spindle is then spun against the thigh with the right hand, and, merrily spinning away, is dropped free, hanging by a bit of wool from the spinner's left hand. The spinner's right hand then pulls more and more wool out of the clump held high above her head with the left hand. Gradually, several feet of spun yarn—the length depends on the distance between the spinner's left hand and the ground under her feet—are created by the rotation of the spindle before it slows down or hits the ground (Illus. 5).

The length of spun wool yarn just created is then wrapped around the spindle, and the entire process is repeated. Wool is

3. Wool being carded with carding comb

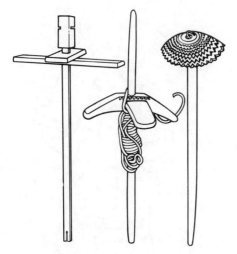

4. Three types of drop spindles

continually added to the clump held in the left hand, then wound around the spindle. Eventually, the spun yarn is removed from the spindle when it becomes too heavy, and is rolled into a ball. Seen under the microscope, wool fibers have a very scaly surface that makes them very easy to spin into yarn, and the creation of yarn from wool appears at first sight to be almost as magical as the creation of a clay vessel on a potter's wheel.

The technique of spinning is taught by mothers to their daughters at an early age. The drop spindle is cheap, easy to use, and highly portable, so spinning can be done while watching children,

*5. Wool being spun by Anatolian
Villagers*

herding sheep, or waiting for the bus. The traditional way of spinning wool used in almost all rug-weaving areas is to spin the spindle *upward* against the thigh with the right hand, imparting a *counterclockwise* spin to the yarn (Illus. 6). When such a yarn is viewed from the side, the lines formed by the fibers make diagonals similar to the middle section of the letter *Z* (Illus. 7). Therefore, we say that yarn spun in a counterclockwise direction has been *Z-spun*. For some reason, perhaps because an upward spin on the thigh is more energy-efficient, the overwhelming majority of spinning done in the rug-weaving world results in Z-spun yarn. Spinning the wool with a *downward* motion of the hand on the thigh would result in clockwise spinning, giving an *S-spun* yarn (Illus. 7); S-spun yarn is only very rarely encountered in a few groups of traditional carpets.

If the reader is beginning to feel a bit dizzy from all of this spinning around, it is important to realize that the ability to

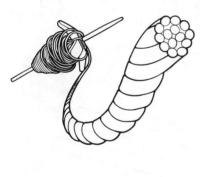

distinguish Z-spun yarn from S-spun yarn is contingent only upon good eyesight and an ability to remember the difference between the letters *Z* and *S*. The yarn so spun is, however, not yet ready to be woven into a rug, because it is too thin and weak. Generally, spun yarns are combined or *plied* into thicker, stronger multi-ply yarns for use in rug weaving. Using a small device that resembles a little spinning wheel (Illus. 8), our spinner becomes a plyer of wool, making a thick multi-ply yarn out of two or more spun yarns. In order for the plied yarn to hold together, it must

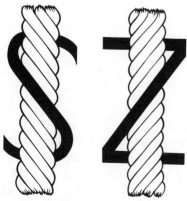

6. *Z-spun yarn attached to spindle*

7. *Diagrams of S-spun and Z-spun yarn*

8. Plying wool using a wheel

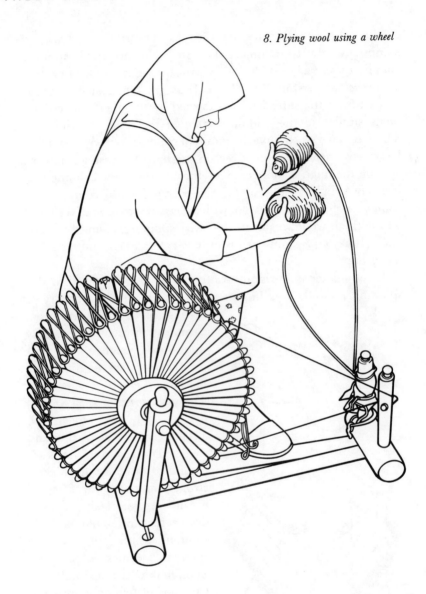

be plied or twisted in the *opposite* direction that it was spun. Thus counterclockwise or Z-spun yarns are always plied together in a clockwise or S-plied manner (Illus. 9). As a principle, in a multi-ply yarn, spin is always the opposite of twist. The wool

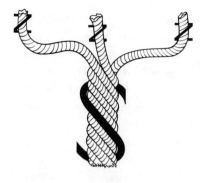

9. Three Z-spun yarns S-plied into a thicker yarn

of white sheep makes the most desirable yarn because it can be dyed in various colors. However, sheep come in many colors, from white to tan to brown to near-black, and for reasons of economy all are shorn and their wool spun and plied into yarn. The wool from the darker sheep may be used to make the warp and weft—the invisible muscles and sinews that we term the *foundation*—of a rug, while the white wool is prepared for dyeing in many colors in order to be used for the visible part of the rug that bears the design.

B. DYEING THE WOOL

Once white yarn has been plied to sufficient thickness and strength in sufficient quantity, the process of dyeing can begin. In traditional weaving of the Middle East, the dyes used to give white sheep wool its brilliant colors are generally made from local materials. (The exception is indigo, used to make blue, which is imported from North Africa.) The most common dyestuff is madder, made from the dried and pulverized root of a common weed found all over Europe and Asia that gives various hues of red, from bright scarlet to dark crimson, eggplant purple and mahogany brown. Yellow often comes from a weed called weld, and black and brown from walnut husks or acorns, sometimes augmented with iron filings. Dyestuffs are placed in a pot of boiling water, usually over a wood fire, and hanks of spun wool are immersed for varying periods of time in the mixture to take on their colors.

Secondary colors are made by dyeing wool twice; green results from dyeing first with weld, then with indigo; and orange may result from using both weld and madder. The dyes themselves are often used in conjunction with a natural material called a *mordant*—a substance that helps the wool to soak up the color of the dyestuff. The most common mordant is alum, a mineral mined from natural deposits, that among other things is used to give crunch to pickles and pucker to trumpet players' lips. Another common mordant is dried and powdered yogurt. Mordants not only help the wool to soak up dye, but may affect the color itself. Depending on the mordant, madder may produce colors ranging from eggplant purple to brick orange.

In general, the longer the wool is left in the dye pot, the deeper the resultant hue. Dyeing with indigo is especially interesting, as the dark blue color appears in the wool *after* the hank is removed from the water; contact with oxygen in the air makes the wool turn from pale yellow to dark blue in a matter of seconds. The hanks of wool, once dyed, are hung from a tree or a fence to dry, and once dried, they are washed to remove excess dye and the powdery residue of the dyestuff.

Rug collectors find knowing about these basic processes extremely useful, because the preparation of materials for weaving is one of the essential determinants of what the final product will look like. For example, the use of traditional dyestuffs and traditional dyeing processes means that no two hanks of wool will be of exactly the same color. The result, in the woven rug, will be subtle variations of color, called *abrash*, that add greatly to the vitality and beauty of a rug. In the later nineteenth century, cheap and easy-to-use industrial dyes from Europe were substituted for the traditional dyes of the rug-weaving world, and the results were often catastrophic. Wool dyed with industrial aniline dyestuffs imported from Germany was often metallic and strident in appearance. Some colors, especially a magenta known as fuchsine, faded rapidly and mercifully to gray after prolonged exposure to sunlight; other colors, especially the reds, were prone to run and stain when the rug was washed. Although rug collectors are in general a kindly and tolerant lot, some of them get grim pleasure on learning that, for a brief period in Persian history, the use of aniline dyestuffs was a capital offense. Today in some parts of the rug-weaving world, there has been a return to the use of traditional dyestuffs that had been employed for many centuries. Most contemporary rug production, however, utilizes yarns dyed with modern chrome dyes that are color- and water-fast and come in a wide variety of hues, but these often lack the warmth and abrash of the traditionally dyed wool.

C. THE LOOM

Once the requisite quantities of wool have been spun, plied, and dyed in appropriate colors, the process of weaving the rug can begin. Although the variations and complications of weaving textiles are enormous, rug-weaving is generally done on very simple looms, and even modern examples are little changed from their ancient prototypes. The simplest kind of loom is a rectangular frame consisting of four pieces of wood, laid flat on the ground or propped up on rocks or logs (Illus. 10). The first step in weaving is to put the *warp,* or the lengthwise yarns that serve as the primary element of the foundation of the rug, on the loom. As it is not ordinarily visible in the final product, the warp may be made of brown wool, or of brown and white wool piled together. Putting the warp on a simple flat loom involves taking a huge ball of yarn, tossing it above the loom, and rolling it back under the loom, gradually wrapping the entire loom with warp yarns (Illus. 10). Thus wrapped, the loom will be used to weave two rugs, one on each side. There are other variations on the basic loom: Some vertical looms are simply flat looms propped up against a wall (Illus. 11); others may utilize roller beams at the top and bottom so that the length of the rug is not limited by the length of the loom (Illus. 12).

The next step in preparing the simple loom for weaving is to separate the warps on one side of the loom into two sets. First, a flat stick, known as a *shed stick,* is threaded above and below each alternate warp yarn across the loom (Illus. 13). When the shed stick is lying flat, the alternate warps are almost on the same level, but when the stick is rotated on its side, a space known as the *shed* is created between upper and lower warps. Now the shed stick is once again rotated to the flat position, and a round pole is placed across the warps that lie *under* the shed stick. This device, the pole and its loops, is known as the *heddle.* When the two-inch-wide shed stick is rotated 90 degrees, it creates a two-inch space called the *shed* between two sets of warps; let's call the upper set

"Set A" and the lower set "Set B." When the shed stick is returned to its flat position (Illus. 14), the warps are again lying
more or less on the same level. When the weaver pulls upward

10. *Wrapping the warp on a simple horizontal loom*

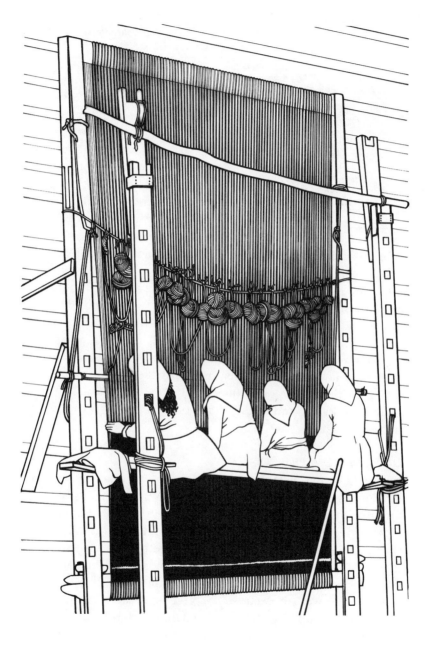

11. Simple vertical loom leaning against a wall, with scaffold to raise weaving bench

12. Roller-beam vertical loom, with large rollers at each end

on the heddle, the result is that the Set B warps *under* the shed stick, which are captured by the loops of the heddle, are pulled *up through* the Set A warps; the lower warps have become the upper warps, and another space has been created (Illus. 15).

The purpose of all of this rigamarole—which is a good deal simpler than it looks, and infinitely simpler in fact than it is in words—is to create spaces through which the lateral "sinews" of the rug, the *weft* yarns, can be passed. By alternately rotating the shed stick and pulling on the heddle, and passing the weft yarn through the spaces so created, the yarns are manipulated into a fabric. If we were to make our fabric only out of warp and weft, and were to pass only one weft yarn through the space every time we rotated the shed stick or pulled the heddle, we would end up with a piece of cloth termed *plain weave*, which would exhibit no design, and would be the color of its constituent warp and weft yarns.

D. WEAVING A PILE RUG

Before the invention of the loom, early rugs were made by pressing large blobs of scoured and carded wool into flat slabs, after wetting it with extremely hot water and highly alkaline soap. Such *felt rugs* (Plate 18) are still made in parts of the world today, and can be made in designs by stitching together cut pieces of different-colored slabs ("mosaic felt") or by sewing thin pieces of felt onto the surface of a thicker slab ("appliqué felt").

However, we are destined for greater or at least for more complex, things: *knotted-pile rugs*. Sometime in the dim and distant past well over three millennia ago, probably in a nomadic encampment in inner Asia, an unnamed tribal weaver invented this new technique. After having woven an inch or two of plain weave

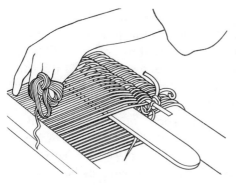

13. Shed stick separating two sets of warps on the horizontal loom

14. Making a heddle, with loops of yarn capturing the warps below the shed stick on a horizontal loom

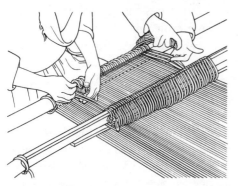

15. Two weavers seated at the horizontal loom

on her loom, inspiration struck: She took the two warp threads at one edge of the loom in her hand, and around them she looped a bit of colored yarn, cutting off the excess with a knife. This resulted in a small tuft of colored wool (we use the term *knot*) sticking up from the surface of her piece of cloth (Illus. 19).

Taking the next two warp threads, she repeated the process. Gifted with great patience, she repeated this process all the way across the loom, creating a thin horizontal row of colored "fuzz" or "pile" on the surface of her fabric. She then rotated the shed stick and passed a weft through the loom. After that, she pulled on the heddle and passed another weft through the loom. Taking a heavy device known as a beating comb, or *comb hammer* (Illus. 18), probably whittled by her cousin out of a heavy piece of wood, she pounded the row of knots and the two wefts down on the loom, and then began the entire process of tying knots again. In an age before television and crossword puzzles, this was probably exciting work. Sometime later (she was a beginning weaver, and thus probably worked very slowly), she reached a point where there was not enough warp left on the loom to continue weaving, and so the first knotted-pile rug was ready to be cut from the loom. This invention was immediately hailed as something very special. With its thick pile, it had all of the insulating characteristics of an animal pelt, but could be woven in colors and patterns like a textile, in a variety of shapes and sizes; it was more durable than felt, and smelled better than animal hides. The simple, patient process just described is the basic technique for weaving knotted-pile rugs, and it has hardly changed at all in the last two-and-a-half to three millennia.

To be sure, there are many variations possible on this basic theme. Although our original weaver probably used a symmetrical knot (Illus. 17B), later weavers in other tribes developed asymmetrical knots opened either to the left (Illus. 17A) or to the right (Illus. 17C). Little did these artists suspect that thousands of years in the future, writers of rug books would coin the nonsensical terms *Gördes knot* and *Sehna knot* to describe, respectively, these symmetrical and asymmetrical knots. Weavers discovered that they had a choice of creating rugs with a long, shaggy pile or a short and very crisp-looking pile. Depending on how slender the warp yarns were and how closely they were wrapped on the loom, a rug could be very coarse (around twenty-four knots in a square inch) or very fine (200 to 2,000 knots in a square inch). As the designs were composed out of thousands and even millions of tiny dots of color formed by the knots, they could be

16. Schematic diagram of slit-tapestry weaving showing the doubling-back of wefts of different colors

either very bold and geometric on a large scale, or very fine and curvilinear on a small scale. The only limit on the size of a rug was the size of the loom. Later, other fibers such as silk, cotton, and metallic wire would be used for rug-weaving. Various complex combinations of warp and weft would be developed, and rugs could be stiff or flexible, thick or thin, shiny or matte, and very coarse or almost incredibly fine, with over 1,000 knots in every square inch.

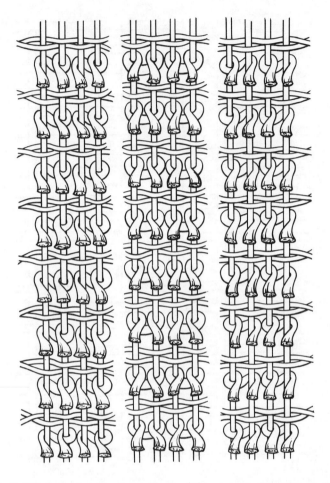

17. A–C: Schematic diagram of carpet knots: (A) asymmetrical knot open to left; (B) symmetrical knot; (C) asymmetrical knot open to right

E. FLAT-WOVEN RUGS

While the knotted-pile carpet is perhaps the most common form of rug encountered today, other techniques have also been used for many thousands of years in the weaving of rugs. The felt rug described earlier, the simplest technique of all, is a *nonwoven* fabric. Rugs woven without pile—we refer to them as *flat-woven rugs* or as *flat weaves*—exist in numerous variants, and readers interested in learning about all of them are referred to in chapter 12 later

18. Various types of comb hammers or beaters used to beat down the wefts and rows of knots on the warps

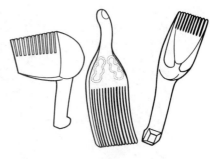

in this book. For our purposes here, we need to be able to recognize two of these flat-weaving techniques. The first is known as *slit-tapestry weaving*, but we will refer to its products as *kilims*. The basic technique of a kilim is plain weave—warps and wefts in even alternation. But in the variant of plain weave known as *weft-faced plain weave* or *tapestry-weaving*, the wefts are pounded down with the comb hammer or weft beater so that they completely cover the warps. In kilim weaving, in order to get beyond a simple design of stripes, different colors of weft are doubled back when they reach the edge of a motif (Illus. 16). The kilim technique therefore creates slits in the fabric where two colors meet along a vertical line, so long, vertical lines in the design are not technically possible. A kind of dovetailing is frequently used as a substitution, and kilim designs, often profoundly influenced by the slit-tapestry technique, often take on a powerful geometric character, with forms that have a power of symbolic suggestiveness that makes Rorschach inkblots quite prosaic and puny in comparison. Kilims are much cheaper to make than pile rugs; they use less material and can be made more quickly. However, their designs are more severely limited by their technique, and they are nowhere near as thick and durable as pile carpets.

To deal with the vexing structural weakness of the slits in kilims, other flat-weaving techniques, known collectively as *brocading*, evolved over time. In brocading, the basic structure of the fabric consists of "structural" warps and wefts, the former all running the full length of the loom and the latter running the full width, exactly as in a pile carpet or in a plain-weave fabric. The design of brocaded rugs is formed by colored *supplementary wefts* woven *on top of* the structural warp and weft, but *at the same time.*

19. Schematic detail of symmetrically knotted carpet

Because the structural wefts, covered up by the supplementary wefts, run from one side of the fabric to the other, there are no slits to weaken the fabric, and straight, crisp vertical lines are possible. Of the many types of brocading, the type known as *sumak* involves supplementary wefts that typically pass over four warps, back under two, over four more, back under two more, and so on (Illus. 20). The sumak and other brocading techniques are much more time-consuming than the kilim, but result in a stronger fabric and allow a greater flexibility in design.

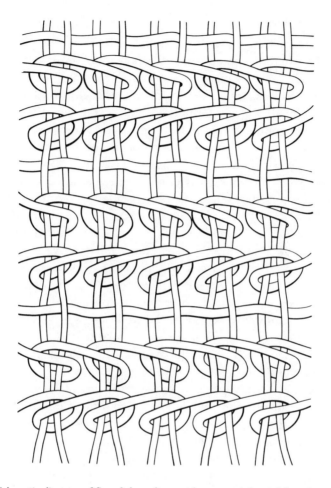

20. Schematic diagram of Sumak brocading, with structural (straight) wefts and decorative (wrapped) wefts

By now, some readers may be wondering what difference exists between brocading, as described above, and the technique of embroidery. In fact, in some cases the end results may be virtually indistinguishable, but in brocading, the supplementary wefts forming the design are *woven on the loom* at the same time as the rest of the fabric. In embroidery, a piece of fabric is woven on the loom and removed, and the design put in afterward *with a needle*.

F. ANALYZING A RUG

If you are by now eager to get to the really interesting material about how to find a bargain at an auction, and how to tell whether or not your rug contains a 10,000-year-old representation of the Mother Goddess, you may legitimately ask why you have been subjected to all of this information about technique. After all, it's the art that counts, right? In fact, the design and color of carpets may constitute the main visual components of the carpet art, but without understanding their technical basis, the collector is in an enormously risky situation. Designs migrate easily from place to place, and a $10,000 Kazak design is readily reproduced in a $200 Hamadan. The Hamadan, however, is woven with only one shot of cotton weft between each row of knots, rather than the customary two. This results in a curiously distinctive back where bits of warp are actually visible while the Kazak has two to four red-dyed wool wefts between each row of knots. The Hamadan's dull pile wool is knotted on cotton warps, while the Kazak's brilliantly shiny wool is knotted on wool warps.

Before you give up completely and turn to stamp collecting, remember that looking at the structure of rugs is 50 percent experience and 50 percent common sense. In my own experience, learning to look analytically at the structure of a rug was far easier than learning to change the tire on a bicycle—and far, far more fun. The best part of knowing how to look carefully at rugs is the wonderful discoveries you can make. These discoveries can sometimes save you from very costly mistakes, and at other times can help you to acquire something for far less than its true value. And they can give you interesting insights into the way human nature operates in the rug market, a subject to be discussed in more detail in chapters 7 and 8 of this book.

When rug experts analyze a carpet for a scholarly catalogue, they follow what by now is a set pattern:

1. First, of course, we look at the design and the colors. Are the colors traditional, with the elegant softening that traditional dyes show over time, or do some of them exhibit either the stridency or the pronounced fading often characteristic of aniline and other industrial dyes? Is the design

clear and understandable as an example of its type? Did the weaver or weavers impart a more or less uniform texture and execution to the fabric? Is it pleasant and interesting to look at?

2. Our next task is to examine the structure of the rug, beginning with a look at the warps. What are they made of, wool or cotton? What color are they? How many plies? How are they twisted together, S or Z? What is the spin of the individual plies, S or Z? Do the warps lie flat and even on the back of the rug, or are alternate warps depressed, resulting in a tighter, stiffer weave and a corduroy-like texture on the back?

3. The wefts: After the material, color, ply, and spin are described, we look at how many times the weft is shot between each row of knots. Rugs with thick bands of weft between each row of knots tend to be coarsely woven; sometimes the color of the weft is essential to determining the rug's place of origin. A close examination of a rug's pattern of wefting once enabled the author to transform a $100,000 seventeenth-century Persian carpet into a nineteenth-century fake in five minutes. It's not as impressive as turning a coach and horses into a pumpkin and mice, but it saved somebody $95,000.

4. The pile: What are the colors, ply, spin, and twist of the pile yarns? What kind of knot is used? Ninety-nine percent of the time, the knot type is absolutely predictable by an expert from the design and other characteristics of the rug. But sometimes, finding a symmetrical knot when you expected an asymmetrical knot open to the right can lead to the discovery of a lifetime, like finding out that your ordinary Yomud camel trapping is a rare and costly Saryk camel trapping. Of much less importance is the density of knotting. The exact number of knots in each square inch of a carpet is of marginal interest to the expert, usually having little bearing on its worth—either artistic or monetary. On the other hand, the *ratio* of knots per inch vertically and horizontally is of enormous interest, because that ratio determines whether a diagonal line in the rug is 45 degrees or steeper, or flatter. Thus, the ratio determines in many cases

the entire appearance of a rug's design, and sometimes, as a consequence, its age relative to that of other rugs.

5. The edges and ends: The structure of the edge of a rug may tell us a great deal about a rug's origin, but more important, it may give information on a rug's condition, as the edges of a rug along with the ends are usually the first parts to show wear. Are borders missing? Is there some trace of an original "skirt" of kilim at each end? Is that cotton fringe original or a machine-made replacement sewn on the rug?

6. The "handle" of a rug: The next step in examining a rug is essentially tactile rather than visual—we might call it determining the "feel" or "handle" of a rug. Is the rug stiff and inflexible, almost like a board? Is it supple and flexible like a handkerchief? Does it feel "meaty" and substantial, or "flabby" and loose? Sometimes the mere tactile response to turning the corner of a rug over with the toe can tell an expert more than fifteen minutes of close-up visual examination.

So you've looked closely at all of these things, and you have determined that the rug before you is a Saryk Türkmen tent bag from central Asia, of respectable age. Are you ready to consider the matter of spending dollars and cents? Not so fast! The last, and most important step of all still lies ahead:

7. Condition and structural integrity: First of all, is the rug all there? Has it been shortened? Has it been narrowed? Or have part of two or more rugs been grafted together? Are borders missing? Are the edges and ends original? Are there any patches grafted in from other rugs?

Now for the colors: Have they been toned down by a chemical bath? Does the rug exhibit a brownish or grayish pallor in the whites indicative of a bath in coffee, tea, or worse? Are there indications of fading in some colors? Look at the roots of the knots for evidence of surface bleach and/ or sunlight fading. Is the pile worn down excessively? Has someone applied the modern miracle of felt-tip markers to mask bare warps and wefts? (This is sometimes referred to in the trade as "enhancement.")

Look at the pile again, this time to see if there is evidence of the depredations of moths, silverfish, or crickets (most rug collectors consider Jiminy Cricket to be a villain in Walt Disney movies). Now examine the rug carefully for splits or tears indicative of dry rot. Remember the story of the two graduate students who went out on their balcony to shake the dust out of their new acquisition and were left with two handfuls of rug; the rest of it, rotten to the core, sailed down to Cambridge Street, where it broke into five pieces. Look once again to see if there has been re-napping or other repair. It is rare to find a good old rug that has not had some repair, but it is best to know what you are getting.

In the vast majority of cases, of course, only a few of these problems will be found in any particular old rug, and the general problems of old age, such as overall wear, raggedy edges and ends, and the depredations of dogs and cats (known to the experts as "widdle marks") are very easy to spot.

The long list we have just gone through may look intimidating. But once again, before you buy that book on stamp collecting, remember two things: First, the kind of knowledge described above comes naturally as one gets better and better acquainted with carpets. Most reputable dealers and auctioneers are scrupulously careful to note problems in a rug's condition; second, consumer legislation provides you with protection after purchase. Many successful collectors can't tell the difference between a symmetrical knot and Knott's Berry Farm, and even some so-called carpet scholars have been known to forget that a knot often makes two little bumps on the back of a rug, and not one.

Again, the watchword is *common sense*. Use your common sense and your eyes. Take as much time as you need; be methodical; seek good and reliable advice; and especially at the outset, don't take expensive chances. As with all kinds of knowledge, knowledge about rugs is acquired gradually and with experience, and the prudent collector doesn't let her reach exceed his grasp, or vice versa. As the Mother Goddess once said to the Tree of Life, "Practice makes perfect."

EARLY CARPET HISTORY

THE PAZYRYK CARPET

The earliest carpet to have survived in substantially intact form was discovered in an underground burial, frozen into a block of ice, by Soviet archaeologists at a site called Pazyryk, located in the Altai mountains of southern Siberia. Forming part of the burial treasure of a nomadic tribal chieftain, the Pazyryk Carpet (Plate 19) is now generally dated to the fourth century B.C.E. ("before the common era"). The Pazyryk carpet was woven using a symmetrical knot (Illus. 19) in exactly the same technique used to weave many of today's carpets. While echoing in some of its designs the contemporary fourth-century B.C.E. Persian art traditions to the south, it was probably woven by central Asian nomads. What is most problematic about the Pazyryk treasure is its uniqueness: There are no other known pile rugs that come from its epoch, and with the exception of a few small fragments and one very enigmatic, crudely designed, and badly faded complete rug—all the products of excavations—the next oldest surviving carpets that can be placed in any kind of artistic context are from around the fourteenth century C.E. This extensive gap in the artistic sequence means that carpet history as documented by a continuous sequence of objects begins only around 1300. The resulting 1,700-year "black hole" of carpet history has also led to the creation of a great deal of speculation, some of it rather harebrained, about an early history of carpets, which has in turn complicated the task of the novice who wants to learn about the genesis and early development of the carpet as an art form.

THE EARLIEST SURVIVING
ISLAMIC CARPETS

While written documents and a few archaeological finds suggest that carpets were produced in the Middle East by many different

Plate 1. "Star Ushak" Carpet, Western Anatolia, 16th Century. Detail, 14′ × 7′7″. The Metropolitan Museum of Art, gift of Joseph V. McMullan, 1958.

Plate 2. Turkish Prayer Rug, Bursa (probably Ottoman period), late 16th Century. 66″ × 50″. The Metropolitan Museum of Art, The James F. Ballard Collection, gift of James F. Ballard, 1922 (22.100.51).

Plate 3. Coupled-Column Prayer Rug, Central Anatolia, 17th Century. 5′6″ × 3′8″. The Textile Museum, Washington, D.C. (R34.22.1).

Plate 4. Lâdik Prayer Rug, Central Anatolia, ca. 1800. 6′1″ × 3′8″. Courtesy of Sotheby's.

Plate 5. Milâs Prayer Rug, Western Anatolia, 19th Century. 5'7" × 3'9".
Private Collection.

Plate 6. Lâdik Prayer Rug, Central Anatolia, ca. 1900. 5'6" × 3'7". The Textile
Museum, Washington, D.C. The Rachel B. Stevens Memorial Collection
(1971.23.10).

Plate 7. Kilim, Central Anatolia, 19th Century. 6′2″ × 5′. Courtesy of Sotheby's.

Plate 8. "Star Kazak" Rug, South Caucasus, 19th Century. 8′2″ × 5′10″.
Courtesy of Sotheby's.

Plate 9. Chechen Prayer Rug, North Caucasus, 19th Century. 5′ × 4′.
Courtesy of Sotheby's.

Plate 10. Heriz Carpet, Northwest Iran, 19th Century. 12′5″ × 10′1″.
Courtesy of Sotheby's.

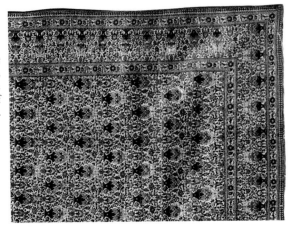

Plate 11. Ferahan Rug in "Zil-e Sultan" Pattern, Arak District, Iran, late 19th Century. Detail. 12′2″ × 8′7″. Courtesy of Sotheby's.

Plate 12. Shah Sevan Sumak *Khorjin* Double Bag, Northwest Iran, late 19th Century. 4′4″ × 1′11″. Courtesy of Sotheby's.

Plate 13. Beluch Rug, Khurasan, Northeast Iran, late 19th Century. Private Collection.

Plate 14. Salor Türkmen Main Carpet, West Central Asia, 19th Century. Detail. 10′9″ × 8′10″.

Plate 15. Ersari Türkmen Main Carpet, West Central Asia, 19th Century. 15′6″ × 7′10″. Courtesy of Sotheby's.

Plate 16. Salor Türkmen *Chuval* Bag Face, West Central Asia, 19th Century. 2′10″ × 4′6″. Courtesy of Sotheby's.

peoples before 1300, the earliest examples surviving from 1300 onward appear for the most part to have been woven by Turkic nomadic peoples and their settled descendants who professed the religion of Islam. These groups migrated westward from central Asia into the Middle East from the middle of the eleventh century C.E. onward. Most of these early carpets seem to have originated in Anatolia, which is today the Asiatic part of the Republic of Turkey, a region with a very complex cultural, ethnic, and religious history; quite a few carpets were found in use as floor covering in mosques—Islamic halls for community prayer— where they seem to have been preserved over the centuries. Their designs reflect origins that can be roughly divided into three groups: (1) a group showing designs of repeating geometric medallions, thought to symbolize the tribe or clan in which the rugs were woven; (2) a group displaying a variety of complex interwoven geometric designs, today known as "arabesque," that share their origins with Islamic architectural decoration and manuscript illumination (Plate 20); and (3) a few examples that show rug weavers copying designs from other civilizations and media, such as a pattern of lotus blossoms adapted from a Chinese silk textile (Plate 21). It is thus highly significant that the earliest rugs to have survived in quantity already show a complex mixture of artistic and cultural origins that the rug medium continues to reflect into our own times.

TRADITIONAL CARPET DESIGNS

By the fifteen and sixteenth century C.E., the carpet historian is on much more secure ground, for by this time carpets from the Middle East were exported in large quantities into Europe, where they were highly valued, and where European painters depicted them very accurately in datable paintings. The easily documented designs of these carpets constitute a large part of the body of traditional designs whose descendants are still used in carpets today. Often known for convenience by the names of European painters, these early carpets are thus enormously important for today's collector interested in the "pedigree" of more recent carpets. Among them are the small-patterned Holbein and Memling carpets (Plates 22, 23), whose small repeating geometric medallions may indicate tribal groups; and the Lotto and large-patterned Holbein carpets (Plates 24, 25), whose overall patterns or large-scale designs share origins with other Islamic media. There are many other common design types in this early group of Islamic carpets, almost all of which have influenced carpet weavers in later centuries. They share the common characteristics of strong primary colors, bold and geometrical designs involving a systematic repetition of basic motifs or patterns, and a clear relationship between the design employed and the rectilinear aspect of the warp and weft upon which the design is knotted.

The Design
Revolution

From around 1450 into the middle of the sixteenth century, these traditional Islamic carpet types were greatly augmented by a third group in a phenomenon known in carpet history as the "design revolution." This artistic revolution resulted from the emerging practice in the Middle East of Islamic rulers founding royal court design workshops centered in or near their capital cities. Designs were created on paper and then sent to workshops to be translated into other media, such as textiles, carpets, metalwork, carvings in wood and ivory, and ornamented arms and armor. The earlier, traditional types of carpets, with their generally coarse knotting, geometric designs, and bold colors based on the four-square technology of the loom, continued to form a major part of the weaving tradition in villages, nomadic encampments, and commercial manufactories. The new carpets, on the other hand, used complex curvilinear motifs and even human and animal figures in their finely knotted fabric, reflecting drawings in pen and ink made by professional court designers and their commercial imitators. Such styles rapidly gained popularity; some court designers even adapted the familiar and popular designs of nomadic carpets to the new style.

Among the new court designs were those reflecting the sixteenth-century imperial taste of the Ottoman Turkish empire, with its capital in Istanbul. Using a subdued color scheme, the Ottoman court carpets reflect popular Turkish designs of whirling stems, curved leaves, and complex palmettes known as *saz*, or stylized tulip and carnation flowers (Plate 26), and sometimes incorporate forms from architectural structure and decoration, such as arches and columns.

From the fifteenth- and sixteenth-century courts and capital cities of Timurid and Safavid in Iran came great medallion carpets (Plate 27), some of them of prodigious size. Their designs, sometimes executed in as many as twenty different colors, recall the decorations of the great tiled domes and painted ceilings of Iranian mosques and palaces. Also from the Iranian capitals of Herat, Tabriz, Qazvin, and Isfahan come carpet designs utilizing human and animal figures, and stemming directly from Persian traditions of miniature painting.

Yet another group of carpets, created for Turkic Mamluk rulers of Egypt and Syria in the fifteenth and sixteenth centuries, utilized an unusual range of colors and rarely encountered S-spun wool (Plate 28). These Mamluk carpets show highly original designs that were distantly inspired by earlier Turkish and perhaps Iranian carpets. Some have suggested that the style of Mamluk carpets was created almost from scratch as a distinctive alternative to Turkish carpets in the Mediterranean markets of the fifteenth and early sixteenth century.

Finally, with the establishment of the Turkic Mughal dynasty in northern India by the end of the sixteenth century, court artists in Delhi and Agra produced uniquely Indian designs for carpets that were sometimes even conceptualized as pictures, with a definite top and bottom, rather than as patterns or motifs viewable from many different angles. The Mughal carpets form a very large group, whose boundaries have not yet been firmly established; many old carpets once thought to have been woven in Safavid Iran, are now thought to have originated in India.

THE CLASSICAL AGE
OF ISLAMIC
CARPETS

By the end of the sixteenth century, the larger part of the traditional design repertory of the carpet medium was already established. From the "classical age" of sixteenth- and seventeenth-century Islamic courts come most of the designs and motifs that today appear in commercial carpets woven the world over. In an attempt to confront the popularity of the court designs, commercial manufactories that had relied on traditional rather than court designs, such as the western Anatolian ateliers in the area of Ushak, had come up with their own innovations. They produced large and striking carpets that used new curvilinear patterns and medallion designs adapted from book illumination and architectural decoration, but utilizing the familiar bright primary colors so beloved of traditional Turkish weavers. During this classical age the cultural embeddedness of the carpet in a wide range of social and economic strata in the Islamic lands of the Middle East was more or less finally established. The next step in the history of the Oriental carpet was the process of cross-fertilization among design types and among social strata, a process that began in the classical age and extends in an unbroken tradition into our own times. In this artistic process two themes emerge that are of great interest to today's carpet collector: For convenience, these may be termed *adaptation* and *stylization*. By adaptation, we mean the process by which a carpet designer or weaver takes a prototype artistic idea—a design or motif—from one work of art and in the process of using it in another work of art, adapts the original idea to the technical limitations of the medium. He or she may also try to fit with the artist's new conception or to harmonize with what the artist has learned as proper standards of color, proportion, or form. Stylization is simply the gradual process whereby generation after generation of adaptations produce, in a particular motif or design, an evolutionary change further and further away from the original prototype.

THE EVOLUTION
OF CARPET DESIGNS
OVER TIME

Both processes can be seen by examining a sequence of carpets. In the late sixteenth century an anonymous designer working at the Ottoman court in Istanbul adapted traditional concepts and motifs to create a new type of carpet design. This designer used traditional *sejjadeh* or prayer-rug dimensions and proportions (about 3½ by 5½ feet) and the traditional Islamic motif of an arch (derived from the Islamic concept of a doorway into Paradise, and also from the architectural niche known as a *mihrab,* indicating the direction to face while praying in a mosque). He also adapted the traditional Islamic symbol for a mosque—an arcade, in this case resting on paired columns—into a novel triple-arched design (Plate 2). In the central arch the artist depicted a hanging lamp, a powerful Islamic symbol for God. The rug employs the characteristic Ottoman palette of eight colors dominated by purple-red, light blue, and medium green wool yarns. Small bouquets of tulips and carnations at the base of the arches symbolize the Heavenly Garden. Sprays of similar flowers, together with complex foliage, make up the border, which is by far the most complicated part of the design. Above the three arches, the artist has depicted four small domes in a parapet of crenellations between which sprout small flowers, today very hard to see against the corroded tan ground. In the spandrels, the white-ground areas between the three arches, we see a delicate arabesque of vegetal forms in dark blue. Finally, the slender columns themselves have tiny leafy capitals at the tops, and their square-faceted polygonal bases appear to have been rendered in perspective.

Every element in this design has been adapted by the male court artist from other sources. In looking at the history of art, it is important to remember the cardinal principle: "Everything comes from somewhere," and to remind ourselves that "originality" in art *always* consists in significant part of artistic transmutations and transformations. The border comes from Ottoman tile designs, themselves resulting from manuscript illumination; the arched format has origins in both Islamic and Judaic religious belief and art; and the architectural motifs were adapted by the artist from known types of Ottoman and Islamic Mediterranean buildings.

This new and original design was then sent to the master of a carpet-weaving atelier, who took the original freehand pen-and-ink design and in effect translated it into a fine graph, with each tiny colored square indicating a single knot of wool yarn. The graph in turn served as a set of instructions for the court carpet-weaver, who then executed the design in a fabric containing roughly 300 asymmetrical knots in every square inch, while having no artistic impact whatsoever on the final product. Thus, we see that this famous early carpet is a collaborative artistic and technical effort on the part of artist/designer, translator, and weaver, supported by all of the labor necessary to produce and dye the yarns making up the carpet.

This one-of-a-kind carpet, perhaps woven to order for the sultan himself, proved to be sufficiently popular that a number of copies were made for commercial sale. By the late seventeenth century, village carpet-weavers became familiar with the type, and adapted it to their own traditions. These female village weavers were artists in every sense of the word: They operated in the context of a tradition, both technical and artistic, passed down from mother to daughter. They were also keen observers of their natural and artistic environment, and they created and adapted designs as an integral part of the weaving process, in marked contrast to the automaton-like weaver of the court carpet. An example of a late-seventeenth-century version of the court carpet, woven with around ninety knots to the square inch, probably in west-central Anatolia, shows the process of adaptation at work (Plate 3).

In this bold and powerful rug, again using eight colors but with more unmixed primary hues dominated by a powerfully intense red, perhaps the most striking adaptation has been the use of a different border. The delicate and complex border of the original and its commercial copies was simply not translatable into the coarser knotting of the village tradition without becoming largely unintelligible. Therefore, a border of small cartouches with highly simplified hyacinths and tulips was substituted; this design adaptation was dictated primarily by technical considerations but also by a different aesthetic that preferred powerful geometrical forms to delicate curvilinear motifs. The other area of great delicacy in the original—the split-leaf arabesque of the arch spandrels—has again been replaced by a simplified rendering of curved, serrated *saz* leaves, and some tiny flowers and stems. It is quite clear that the complex shape of the blue-ground spandrel area was the most problematic for the village weaver.

In the parapet above the arches, the domes have been omitted, the number of crenellations reduced, and the hard-to-read blossoms of the original have been replaced by a row of much larger geometric flowers. And finally, the architecture of the original has been drastically modified. The semicircular arches of the court rug, easy to execute in a finely knotted carpet, have been replaced by gables at a 35-degree angle, which accurately reflects the horizontal-to-vertical ratio of roughly nine to eleven knots per inch. In addition, the central arch has been given great prominence. Lastly, the columns have been drastically simplified into decorative stripes with abbreviated capitals and bases, suggesting that the resemblance between the carpet design and actual architecture was of little if any significance to the weaver.

Most if not all of the adaptations from the sixteenth-century court carpet observable in the late-seventeenth-century village rug are in the direction of simplified form, but also result in a more elemental and powerful visual impact. Both of these differences may be attributable not only to a different set of technical and material circumstances, but to a different set of artistic ideals. The result of this process repeating again and again, generation after generation, is *stylization*—a process in which forms not only become progessively more simplified, but may in fact evolve into alternative forms with other meanings. For example, a leaf may ultimately turn into a bird, or vice versa.

There is one other aspect of the village carpet that is important to consider, however, and this is the order in which parts of the carpet were woven. The order can be determined by simply stroking the pile, a physical act that immediately informs the stroker that the actual *bottom* of the rug, the end from which weaving was begun, is at the *top* of the illustration. The direction of the pile points toward the end with the tops of the arches, just as the direction of fur on the back of a cat points toward the tail. In a rug executed from a set of written instructions or from a graphed design, it makes very little difference artistically from which end the weaver begins. But in the case of a weaver who is to some extent creating the design as she weaves the rug, this may have much greater significance. For what reasons did the weaver of this rug begin her labors at the top, rather than the bottom, of the design—and what are some of the effects of this process?

A first possibility is that while she may have found the design of the original to be attractive, the weaver did not recognize the architectural nature of the design. Assuming that her design was adapted from an example fairly close to the original, however, this is unlikely. A far more likely reason is the fact that the upper end of the rug, as illustrated, is far more complex than the lower. Since the weaver used a small vertical loom about six feet high, and the rug itself is almost exactly five-and-a-half feet long, the weaver may have made a practical decision to weave the complicated part of the rug, which is the most difficult and the least adaptable to having its dimensions altered, at the beginning of the weaving process. Approaching the top end of the loom at the end of the process, it was very easy to terminate the columns with simple bases and start the horizontal border. Here, however, she decided to experiment with a different kind of corner adjustment, and the result was a border with partial cartouches on each side, and some compromises at both corners. Artistic solutions to the "corner problem" are among the most interesting and varied evidences of the artistic process, with its inevitable triumphs and failures, adaptations and compromises, risks and experiments, that one sees in village carpets. It is a revealing insight into the very core of the process of art—"art in the raw"—unconcealed by an extra layer of paint, an extra handful of clay, or the application of sandpaper or a burnishing tool to the surface of an engraver's plate.

And now, let us suppose that for the sake of argument the

village carpet we have just examined, created in west-central Anatolia, was somehow sold to a buyer from Konya province, who as an act of piety gave it to his local mosque in the small town of Lâdik. There, sometime in the late eighteenth century, it was seen by a local weaver who, like her earlier counterpart in west-central Anatolia, had probably seen and vaguely remembered a commercial copy of the original court rug, but who was particularly struck by the design of the later village rug. Returning to her loom, she began work on her own version of the design (Plate 4). Her rug was a typical Lâdik product, with the alternatively depressed warps characteristic of the region, only five colors, and a coarser weave, with a ratio of six knots per inch horizontally to nine vertically, producing an even flatter diagonal.

In the Lâdik product, which today is missing knots from both ends, the weaver had dimly remembered those faceted bases from the columns of the original court rug, and reproduced them as a series of little squares ornamented by single dots of color. Not having the remotest idea of what a column was, she turned the outermost column bands of the west Anatolian rug into vaguely shrublike forms in white and blue. Not having the remotest idea of the appearance of coupled columns or a triple arcade, she expanded the space between the columns in each pair, and turned the central arch into a very narrow panel. She made a very simple adaptation of the border of the other village rug, and connected her cartouches by a white stripe, inserting a series of random ornaments into the ground of the border and the spandrels. Unlike her wiser and more disciplined village predecessor, she unfortunately began the rug at the bottom of the design, but ran out of loom before she could weave blossoms on top of the stems at the top of the rug, leaving naked stems as a testament to her lack of foresight. However, profiting from the awkward corner adjustments of her predecessor, she made a crude but effective border turn at each top corner of her rug. Her rug is disorderly, even reckless, but it has wonderful colors, and an inventive charm all of its own. Through the process of stylization, the Lâdik rug is now even more distant from its ancestor in the Istanbul court.

Finally, let us imagine that this Lâdik rug was sold to a traveler from northwest Anatolia, who took it home to his village near the modern town of Bergama and gave it to his grandson. Sometime in the first half of the nineteenth century, a weaver from the same village saw it on the floor of the grandson's modest village house. This weaver, no doubt born between August 20 and September 21, and possessed therefore of a neat and orderly mentality that in a later century would have assured her of an editorial post at Sotheby's, was as repelled by the disorderly aspect of the Lâdik rug as she was intrigued and excited by the basic design, and so she got out her loom and produced a version of her own (Plate 29).

The weaver of this fourth variation on the fundamental theme of the triple-arched prayer rug had a great respect for symmetry, both horizontal and vertical, and therefore dispensed with the spindly columns of the prototype in favor of reproducing the complex end of the rug twice, in mirror image. There are three arches up and three arches down, and the white-ground spandrels are filled with orderly rows of geometric motifs long used in the weaving tradition of the local area. There is a neat row of flowers on a parapet pointing down at the bottom of the rug, and a similar row up at the top, but the latter row and the border above it have been somewhat squashed, again probably in an attempt to get everything into the available space on the loom. Our admirable Virgoid artist used a dramatic local border with brown-black ground, filled with a beautiful array of simplified blossoms in varicolored simple cartouches, and by the artful augmentation of the blank space in the lower right-hand border, managed an initial corner resolution that she was even able to improve upon at the top of the rug. Intrigued by a date she saw woven into an earlier Lâdik rug that had been given to the local mosque (1182 Hegira, corresponding to 1768 C.E.), she copied it into her own rug, not once but four times. The result of her labors, with its brilliant colors, powerful design, and ingenious adaptation of motifs, is artistically at least as compelling as the sixteenth-century original, albeit for an almost entirely different set of reasons. The gradual process of stylization has resulted in yet another powerfully original work of art, this time from the early nineteenth century.

COLLECTIBLE CARPETS
OF THE
18TH–20TH CENTURIES

As we have seen, the transmission of design traditions and the introduction of design innovations in carpet history occur both "horizontally" (in time, as designs are passed from one generation of weavers to the next) and "vertically" (as designs are transmitted from one level of society to another, or from one part of the weaving world to another). By the seventeenth century C.E. three distinctive court carpet traditions, each to some extent influencing the others, were flourishing in the Ottoman Turkish, Safavid Persian, and Mughal Indian empires of the Middle East. At the same time, parallel nomadic, village, and commercial carpet traditions were also in existence, and all of these traditions to one extent or another interacted either economically or artistically with the others. In the seventeenth and eighteenth centuries C.E., all three of the great Islamic empires underwent political and economic decline, partially for internal reasons and partially because of European expansion. In 1683 the collapse of the Ottoman Turkish siege of Vienna led to a prolonged retreat from Eastern Europe, which aggravated serious internal economic problems in the Turkish realms. In 1722 the Safavid dynasty in Persia collapsed in the face of an invasion by the Afshars from Afghanistan under Nadir Shah, and the virtual disappearance of centralized political authority led to a similar debacle in the economy of Persia. In India, the Mughal dynasty lost control of the subcontinent to the colonizers of the British East India Company.

In Europe, the taste for Oriental carpets had become established in the fifteenth century, as carpets came to symbolize wealth, power, and sanctity. That finally changed by the end of the seventeenth century, in large part because of the new concept of unity of style in the decorative arts originating in court patronage under Louis XIV of France. With the royal Savonnerie, Gobelins, and Sèvres manufactories of France producing furniture, tapestries, carpets, and ceramics in the prevailing Baroque style, and with the once-powerful Eastern empires now the subject of curiosity and satire, rather than fear and respect, the popularity of the Oriental carpet began to fade in Western Europe. Nevertheless, it continued unabated in the central European lands, especially in Austria, Hungary, and Romania. At the same time, with the restriction or elimination of court patronage and the collapse of the economies of the great Islamic powers, carpet production declined drastically in the Middle East, although it continued to flourish among nomadic peoples in central Asia and remained a part of the fabric of everyday life in many villages and encampments in the traditional "rug belt."

By the mid-nineteenth century, a multitude of factors contributed to a revival in production of Oriental carpets. One of these was the "internationalizing" of European taste in the age of colonialism, when Europeans became aware of the artistic production of faraway places through travel and colonial adventures. Then began the serious collecting of art from non-European traditions by the great national museums of fine and applied arts that became an essential cultural accoutrement of a modern European nation. Another contribution to this internationalizing of taste, stemming from the same causes, was the phenomenon of Orientalism in European art, especially in painting, where Islamic themes, notably those of the harem, were accompanied by an interest in the "props" of exotic Oriental societies. Reaction to European economic imperialism brought about an encouragement of export industries by a few Eastern countries, and this often included the indigenous carpet industry.

TURKEY

The Hereke imperial manufactory near Istanbul was founded in 1843. The institution simultaneously produced "modern" textiles with power looms, and sponsored a revival of carpet-weaving for the court, much of it unfortunately in a Europeanized style then in vogue in the Ottoman Empire. The fashion for Turkish carpets in Europe, especially in the popular *sejjadeh* format, led to a production in the west Anatolian centers of Gördes and Kula of small carpets designed to appeal to the European taste for pastel colors and fussy designs. The production of Ushak revived, concentrating on "room sized" carpets in European formats rather than the classical long rugs for which Ushak had long been famous. In Istanbul, in the Kum Kapı ("Sand Gate") quarter, a limited production of very finely knotted rugs in a classical Persian style flourished for a few decades.

TRANSCAUCASIA

In the Caucasus, an area which has seen a limited commercial production of carpets from the seventeenth century onward, local Islamic weavers adapted Iranian designs from Kerman, and their handiwork spread as a result of the entrepreneurship of Armenian and foreign merchants. By the late nineteenth century, there was a dramatic increase in production for export, encouraged by the Russian rulers and characterized by a huge production of small carpets by Turkic weavers in the south and east Caucasus. These carpets used a complex variety of local designs and weaving techniques that seemed to have survived through the previous century in a limited production on the village and tribal level. Largely destined for export, many of these rugs were characterized by original and interesting adaptations of individual motifs from earlier Caucasian and Anatolian carpets. Many unfortunately used aniline dyes or were subjected to chemical baths that altered their color in order to enhance their attractiveness in the marketplace.

IRAN

In Iran, the revival of commercial weaving, first in the city of Tabriz in the far northwest, and then under the aegis of Tabrizi merchants in Kerman and other centers in the south, rapidly came under the domination of a few large companies. Many of them were European-based, and they supplied the flourishing markets of Western Europe and North America with a large variety of Iranian carpets, mostly in the larger "room size" formats, or as runners for corridors and stairways. The acquisition of great examples of classical Iranian weaving by major European museums, and especially the acquisition of the famous Ardebil Carpet (Plate 27) by London's Victoria and Albert Museum in 1888, lent new prestige and cachet to the large Iranian carpets, which were *de rigueur* floor coverings for the great country houses of England and for the equally sumptuous urban palaces erected by America's financial and industrial elites. India likewise experienced a revival in production of large carpets, although British economic policy and distance from European and North American markets kept Indian production from becoming a serious rival to the carpets produced in Iran.

The age of imperialism affected carpet production in different ways in different parts of the world. By destroying the political and social structure of the Türkmen tribes of central Asia, the Russian conquest brought one of the world's richest and oldest weaving traditions to an end, although the conquerors to some extent documented the dying weaving traditions with collections amassed by military officers and later given to Russian museums. French colonialism in North Africa, especially Morocco, resulted in some cases in expanded production of local rugs for export to metropolitan France. And the virtual takeover of the export economy of China by foreigners also led to a revival of European interest in Chinese carpets, which were rarely seen and consequently little understood or appreciated in the West before the late nineteenth century.

Carpet-weaving in the major carpet-producing areas in our own time will be included as a part of our discussion of each area. It is important to remember, however, that what makes the carpet so unusual as an art form is the long and unbroken history of design stretching back in history; carpets are a living art form, but part of their attractiveness to collectors stems from their deep and complex roots in a colorful, historic past.

WHY PEOPLE
COLLECT CARPETS

Given the fundamental nature of the collecting impulse in human history, it is reasonable to suppose that there have been carpet collectors as long as there have been carpets to collect. Documents about early collectors, such as Cardinal Wolsey in early-sixteenth-century England, indicate that the phenomenon of compulsive acquisition of art—what some today refer to as "white-knuckle collecting"—has been around for a long time. Collecting in the modern sense, however, began in the late nineteenth century, as both museums and wealthy middle-class patrons began to emulate European aristocratic tastes. Also at this time, dealers such as Joseph Duveen began to market great classical Islamic carpets, especially the masterpieces of court weaving from the Ottoman, Safavid, and Mughal empires, as worthy works of art on the same plane as old-master paintings. The appearance of rug literature— much of it unfortunately not very accurate or informative— served as another impetus to collecting. Finally, the attention of major historians of art, such as the Viennese theorist Alois Riegl and the founder of the Berlin Museums, Wilhelm von Bode, brought a new measure of respect to the serious collecting of "classical" carpets, especially those that were often depicted in old-master paintings of the Renaissance and Baroque periods.

The artistic relationship between the great antique masterpieces and more recent Oriental carpets did not go unnoticed by a number of important collectors who built up collections between the World Wars. The great American collectors George Hewitt Myers, James Ballard, and Joseph V. McMullan acquired both classical carpets and their more recent descendants. The New York Hajji Baba Club, the first North American rug collector society, was formed in 1932 under the energetic leadership of the dealer/scholar/poet Arthur Urbane Dilley; its middle-class members came from the professions and the business world. But it was not until the late 1950s that the modern collecting phenomenon as we know it today first began to take off. It was fueled by a series of landmark exhibitions at such institutions as Harvard's Fogg Art Museum in Cambridge, Massachusetts, and New York's Asia Society, and urged on by such figures as McMullan, who became a mentor to a new generation of collectors.

For some collectors in the fifties and sixties, the combination of powerful design and low market prices found in flat-woven rugs (until then relatively ignored by collectors and dealers) resulted in a specialization in these weavings. Besides the attractive prices, the excitement of pioneering an unpublished and unknown area has resulted in the development of many important new areas of collecting, such as south Persian nomadic pieces, the Beluch tribal rugs of east Persia, city rugs of east central Asia, and the tribal rugs of Moroccan Berbers or Kurds from Iraq, Iran, and Turkey. Some collectors have focused on particular genres of rugs, such as animal trappings or small utility bags.

The influence of publications has been enormous. In 1958 the color illustration of a particular type of south Caucasian rug popularly known as an Eagle Kazak on the cover of a pioneering exhibition catalog from the Asia Society contributed to this type of rug commanding, for almost a decade, a price much higher than that of any comparable rug type from the Caucasus. The publication of Ulrich Schürmann's encyclopedic *Caucasian Rugs* in German and then in English in the 1960s gave names to many different design types. While collectors were often reluctant to buy what they could not name, the sudden and miraculous appearance of Karagashli, Perepedil, Konagend, and Seichur in the lexicon, linked to the attractive color illustrations in Schürmann's book, led to a marked increase in "color-plate collecting" of rugs with similar types of designs.

In contemporary collecting there are many different tastes and many different emphases, which are worth examining if we are to learn from the successful collector of today. Some collectors develop at the outset an aesthetic preference for the weavings of a particular geographic area: The finely woven and precisely designed city rugs of Iran may appeal to some, while others may prefer the brilliant coloration of Anatolian rugs; still others may find the effect of the red-hued Türkmen rugs of central Asia to exert an almost hypnotic fascination. At the outset, many collectors develop a basic preference for either more rough-hewn, single-artist nomadic and village rugs or the collaboratively created, exquisitely planned and executed city weavings.

Today, several phenomena fuel rug collecting and determine areas of collector interest, and they deserve mention before we look at the rugs themselves.

1. The first, and by far the most important, is the relatively low price of carpets in comparison to other works of art with

similar levels of visual appeal. Crudely put, for many lovers of beautiful things, rugs give a far bigger aesthetic bang for the buck. Once the rise of abstract expressionism and its successors established the principle that something hung on a wall can be beautiful without depicting recognizable objects or beings, then the Perepedil became a serious alternative to the Pollock, and the Kazak's appeal was no more mysterious than that of the de Kooning.

2. A second factor, of course, is the rise in knowledge about carpets, itself a product to a significant degree of private collecting and exhibitions drawing heavily on private collections. The combination of practical function and visual beauty, when set in a context of ethnography, anthropology, geography, and cultural myths and realities, is for many collectors almost irresistible, and the explosion in the rug literature, while it has serious drawbacks, has certainly added an intellectual dimension to those of visual excitement and the acquisitive urge.

3. A third factor is the widespread perception that collecting rugs is a good investment. The reason why this perception is especially important in the area of rug collecting is that it helps to overcome the two factors that are traditionally the major brakes on the collective urge: lack of confidence, and guilt. In successful rug collecting, confidence in one's judgment and taste must exceed the fear of risk. The popular perception that, as a whole, the market continues to rise makes the risk seem far less, and builds collector confidence. Likewise, guilt at spending on a work of art a sum one might instead give to charity, or set aside for a child's college education, can always be conveniently assuaged by telling oneself, however dishonestly, that the expense is an investment."

4. The fourth factor in making carpet collecting an attractive option is a level playing field between the academic "expert" and the serious collector. The relatively recent serious interest in the nineteenth-century carpets that form much of the focus of collector interest, together with the often mediocre scholarly quality of many rug publications, means that significant discoveries are still to be made. A serious

collector who is not a historian of art may in fact be able to make a substantial discovery that is an important contribution to knowledge.

5. The fifth and last factor, not related to the fourth, that makes carpet collecting attractive to many people is the atmosphere of myth and mystique that surrounds so many of these hand-made, one-of-a-kind objects themselves. In a society where we are surrounded by things that are mostly new and almost totally the product of industrial manufacture, carpets present us with a tangible tie to faraway places and distant times, and they bring with them the aura of the Mysterious East that has been an important part of what we call "Western" culture for hundreds of years. From the collector who believes his precious bag face to have been woven for the dowry of a Türkmen princess, to the owner of a fragmentary Turkish kilim who sees in an ambiguous geometric form the image of the great prehistoric Mother Goddess, carpets by their often very ambiguous forms and uncertain origins help to satisfy a very real need for contact with the historical past and with the broader human world of artistic and spiritual accomplishment. Sometimes, when the more bizarre of these fantasies and longings appear in print masquerading as serious scholarship, they can be either infuriating or humorous, or both.

More often than not, the complex human motivations for collecting lead to the sharing of knowledge, pleasure, and enthusiasm for objects of wondrous beauty. All of this helps expand our awareness of universal human values that easily transcend cultural boundaries.

NAMES AND CATEGORIES OF CARPETS

In focusing on the carpets themselves, we have chosen for reasons of broad inclusiveness to use geography, rather than ethnicity, as the basis for our most fundamental categories. But at the outset, we need to ask ourselves the old question, "What's in a name?" The names (and consequently the categories) we impose on rugs are of several types. Some prefer to use ethnic terms such as Turkish, Persian, Caucasian, and Türkmen instead of the geographic names used in this book: Anatolia, Iran, Transcaucasia, and central Asia. Within these broad categories many carpets bear city or town names, like Lâdik, Kerman, or Kuba. Sometimes groups of carpets are known by names of broad tribal or ethnic weaving groups like Yörük (the Turkish word for "nomad"), Türkmen, Kurd, Berber, or Beluch. Sometimes they are identified by the names of very specific tribal groups, such as Afshar, Akhal Tekke, Turbat-i Haidari, or Yüncü. Sometimes carpets are named according to use: *ensi* ("door-hanging"), *yastık* ("pillow"), *namzlík* ("for prayer") or *sejjadeh* ("for prostration"). Sometimes the names are derived from descriptions of the designs or motifs on a rug: *hatchli* ("with a cross"), *kedi paça* ("cat's footprint"). All too often the terms we use are misnomers: *Bukhara rugs* for Türkmen rugs, *Bergamo rugs* for rugs that were sold at markets in Bergama, or *Laver Kerman* for rugs thought to have been woven in the town of Raver in Kerman province. And last of all, there are faulty names resulting from the mistranscription of terms from Asian languages into French or German, and thence into English: among these are the Anglo-Saxon "Yarmouth" instead of the more exotic "Yomud" (a Türkmen tribe), the Gallic "Monjour" for "Mujur" (an Anatolian village), the peculiar ornithological invention "osmulduk" (a rare bird indeed) for "asmalyk" ("hanging"), or even the relatively harmless "Ghiordez" for the western Anatolian town of Gördes. In this vein I am fond of recalling the collector whose pride was a beautiful Bilmem rug; the name resulted from his asking an Istanbul dealer where the rug came from. The honest response was: *"Bilmem"*—"I don't know."

CHAPTER 3

*W*HAT ARE ANATOLIAN CARPETS?

INTRODUCTION

We will begin with Anatolian carpets, often called Turkish carpets, the first group to appear in the West in the late Middle Ages and still a major area of collector interest today. The geography and ethnology of Anatolia (Map 2) and southeastern Europe, where these rugs were originally woven, are very complex. The country we call Turkey came under Turkish rule less than a thousand years ago, as nomadic tribes from Inner Asia migrated westward under the leadership of the Seljuks. The successors of the Seljuks, the Ottoman dynasty, established itself in Anatolia around 1300, and by the end of the sixteenth century ruled an empire stretching from the outskirts of Vienna to Baghdad, and from Libya to the Crimea. Because orthodox Islam, as professed by the ruling Turkish dynasties, dictates a policy of tolerance for "people of the book"—Christians and Jews—the Ottoman Empire flourished as a multiethnic state in which many different peoples contributed to a distinctive and complex Ottoman culture under a Turkish and Islamic political and cultural umbrella. But while, as we have noted, historical sources indicate that rug-weaving existed in parts of Anatolia before the coming of the Turks, the surviving artistic record suggests very strongly that the prevailing style in weaving since the fourteenth century stemmed from a Turkic culture with roots in a nomadic central Asian past. Simply put, in the complex ethnic mixture of Anatolian villages and cities, most rug-weaving was an important part of the dominant culture.

THE "TRADITIONAL PROVENANCE"
RUGS OF ANATOLIA

Anatolian rugs defy any easy attempt at categorization. Apart from the early "classical" rugs of the types depicted in European paintings—the Holbeins and Lottos, Memlings and Crivellis—collectors have traditionally been interested in a series of Anatolian rug groups that we call the "traditional provenance groups." These tend to be fairly small in size, with a fairly large preponderance of *sejjadeh,* or prayer carpets. Four examples of such carpets were illustrated earlier in our discussion of adaptation and stylization. They embody particular techniques and designs that we can easily link to particular towns or villages; thus the group names are virtually all town names. These vary widely, from the once-popular products of Kula and Gördes, with their fussy, detailed designs and subdued colors designed with Western customers in mind, to the carpets of Milâs, near the Aegean coast, with their brilliant and warm traditional colors, soft wool, red wefts, and designs that often display in their spandrels stylized lotus flowers that are direct descendents of sixteenth-century forms (Plate 5). The Gördes weavings often show on the back faint zigzag lines that indicate that the weft was often not passed all the way across the rug, but turned back on itself. Some Gördes rugs, exploiting the advantages of this practice, use a light-colored weft under light areas of the design, and a dark-colored weft under the dark areas, so that wear will be less visible.

Of different construction and design are the rugs of northwest Anatolia that used to be collectively known in the market under the name Bergama, a Turkish town on the site of ancient Pergamon where some of these rugs evidently used to reach the market. This group of rugs in particular often shows strong ties to the classical Turkish carpets of the fifteenth century, such as the large-pattern Holbeins. It is now possible to localize both town and tribal groups within the area of northwest Anatolia, and the depth of local traditions has led to two areas, Ayvajik (Ayvacık) and Yuntdağ, being chosen as sites for the revival of traditional designs and dyeing methods in our own time.

A number of Anatolian prayer rugs show close family resemblances; the Mujur (Mucur), Kırshehir (Kırşchir), and Lâdik prayer rugs (Plates 5, 30), for example, all incorporate a stepped "arch" at the top, which appears in this particular instance to be modeled on the distinctive type of *mihrab* or prayer niche denoting the direction of Mecca used in Turkish mosques. All were woven near each other in central Anatolia. But their weaving structures are quite different, as are their colors, their local traditions of borders and ornamental motifs, and even their proportions, although to make things even more confusing, sometimes a Mujur weaver copied a Kırshehir rug, or vice versa. Avidly collected for over a hundred years, fine examples of these types are both expensive and hard to find.

The designs of these central Anatolian cousins are to one extent or another all descendants of the sixteenth-century Ottoman court rugs, but their characters are quite distinctive. The sober Lâdiks, stiff and strongly constructed, with highly individual corner adjustments, are more finely knotted and apparently have an older lineage. In Lâdiks, the two main areas of the rug field, the "niche" and the "crenellation panel" are often combined quite

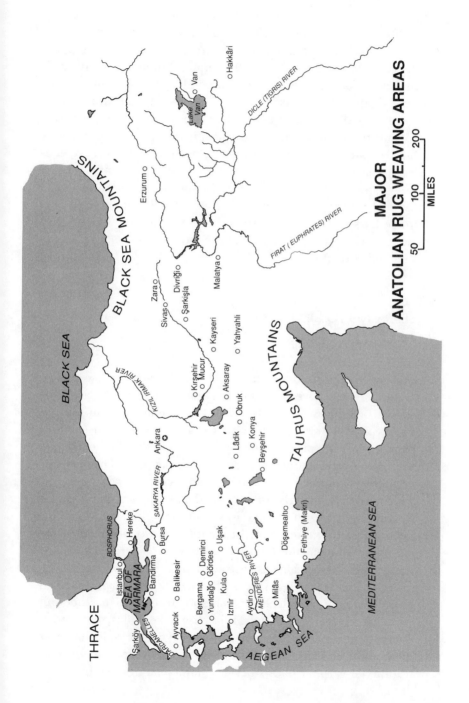

arbitrarily in a variety of relationships, right-side-up and upside-down. Many old examples bear Hegira dates roughly corresponding to 1790–1800 c.e. The loose, supple Mujur rugs, with their ingenious border adjustments, are almost invariably woven "upside-down" for reasons we have discussed, and Mujur weavers are fond of using the motif of a ewer or water pitcher at various places on the rug. Most Mujur rugs are woven in a very limited range of basic design types, but the variations are endlessly fascinating. The even looser and, from the point of view of design, more diverse early Kırshehir prayer rugs show an almost astonishing range of colors (including a traditional mauve) that made Kırshehir weavers sitting ducks for the first aniline dyes. Later Kırshehir rugs are among the most unfortunate victims of the aniline blight.

Learning to Develop
Standards Within Groups

For the most part, Anatolian carpets within each of these groups, and other groups we have not been able to discuss here, are fairly similar in design and construction. But learning the basic features of a typical example (and our illustrations have been carefully chosen to show typical features) does not in itself help the collector to make discriminating choices in the marketplace The next step is to look at a number of examples from each group "in the wool." This is not particularly difficult for the novice, for such rugs are frequently displayed in exhibitions and are often discussed and illustrated in the literature. In identifying Anatolian rug types, it is best to avoid the tendency to rely on general elements of design, which were sometimes traded back and forth. Rather, the collector should concentrate on the significant design details—and the weight, suppleness, wool, and structure—that not only allow us to distinguish the Mujur from the Milâs, but also to recognize the merely interesting or typical carpet as distinct from the fine work of art. We are also better able to separate the older traditional carpet from its newer commercial descendant.

The coming of industrial dyes to Anatolia in the second half of the nineteenth century led to the decline in quality of all of these traditional types, a decline we can see very easily by comparing a Lâdik rug of around 1900 with its predecessor woven over a century before (Plate 4). The design in most of its aspects is almost identical: The field with its stepped arch, the main borders with their characteristic flattened rosette and sprig of stylized tulips, the panel with crenellations and flowers, and the weaver's tendency freely to arrange the major elements that she has inherited through many generations from the sixteenth-century classical Ottoman court prototype. The major difference is in color: The purple faded to gray, the dark orange faded to tan, and the generally weak and subdued palette of the later carpet, however well these may match up with the sofa or the drapes, are the sure sign of a tradition in serious artistic decine. The loose and flabby weave, lifeless wool, and irregular wefting of the later example confirm the evidence of the bad colors and the blurring and weakening of the precise earlier design—a loss for which the addition of geometric decoration in the field is poor compensation. Some novices make the serious mistake of trying to acquire "types" from the beginning, rationalizing that "half a Lâdik is better than none." Most experienced collectors would agree that it is a waste of collecting time and resources to buy a substandard example of any type, and that acquiring for type alone neither enriches one's collection nor one's knowledge.

New Anatolian Frontiers

By the time that the contemporary collecting boom began, older examples of the "traditional provenance" Anatolian rugs were already well known and very expensive, and the later examples from the same places were not of serious interest to collectors. In their place, a new group of rugs had arisen, mostly in the twentieth century, and also firmly associated with places. Among these were Kayseri, Taşpinar, and Yahyahlı weavings, primarily executed with colorfast but untraditional chromium dyes, and in the case of the Kayseri rugs, largely severed from their historical past. Their major advantage was that each had a name and a secure provenance, but again knowledgeable collectors largely ignored them because their colors and designs neither appealed to those familiar with the great historical examples, nor to those seeking interior decoration in the current mode.

Instead, by the sixties, collectors began to find out that the world of Anatolian weavings of the nineteenth century was incalculably more vast than the well-known but limited group of "traditional provenance" carpets.

1. Kilims of Anatolia   First of all, collectors discovered kilims. These slit-tapestry-woven Turkish pieces, while always known, were low in status because no one knew where they were woven— and they were, after all, "only kilims." They lacked pile, so they were "missing" something important. Furthermore, because they were quite fragile and, although simple in structure, paradoxically very difficult to repair in an unobtrusive fashion, older examples in intact form were hard to find. However, the old examples did have marvelous colors, and the extremely bold and large-scale designs, dictated in part by the technique itself, were quite compelling (Plate 7). An exhibition circulated by The Textile Museum in 1969, entitled "From the Bosphorus to Samarkand: Flat-Woven Rugs," can be credited in large part with provoking the kilim boom, as well as a renewed interest in sumak and other types of brocaded weaving. In fifteen years, the lowly kilim became the hottest part of the Anatolian collecting scene. A number of very early kilims using classical Ottoman designs showed up, some of them discovered in isolated Anatolian village mosques. A London dealer, Yanni Petsopoulos, published a huge tome entitled *Kilims* that accomplished for these nameless flat-woven rugs what Ulrich Schürmann's *Caucasian Rugs* had done for its subject a decade before. Turkish kilims, as well as those from other parts of the rug world, were grouped according to their broad geographical origins, and then given names. Reyhanlı and Obruk moved from the rarefied world of a few connoisseurs and dealers into the carpet mainstream. A new wave of exhibitions followed, together with studies that attempted to prove that the large-scale, powerful, almost totemic designs of many Turkish kilims had artistic links to an Anatolian past that went back many millennia. It looked as if kilims, in addition to having become artistically respectable, were gaining an intellectual pedigree as well. As older pieces were stripped from Turkish mosques by dealers seeking to feed the hungry marketplace, suddenly half-kilims, kilims with holes, and even small fragments of kilims began to bring high prices. Even the unmasking of outright scholarly fraud in a major publication on the subject failed to dampen the enthusiasm of the market. The ancient Mother Goddess of Anatolia, whom many enthusiasts claimed to see represented in the bold geometric forms of old Anatolian kilims, had once again become the object of religious rather than scientific attention.

The excesses of kilim enthusiasts notwithstanding, the new collector focus on kilims had several highly positive results. First, almost unnoticed in the Mother Goddess furor, serious incremental gains in historical knowledge about kilims have begun to emerge. Second, because of their rise in status and price, old kilims of stupendous beauty and power are now being respected and preserved in private collections and in museums, rather than being worn out or discarded.

2. New Types of Early Pile Carpets   In addition to kilims, there are three other newly emergent areas of serious collector interest in older Anatolian rugs. As the two great Istanbul carpet museums, the finest collections of Turkish rugs in the world, began to exhibit on their walls old carpets of types other than the "usual suspects"—the familiar classical pieces and the "traditional provenances"—collectors quickly became aware that there was an immense variety of early pile weaving from Anatolia that was little understood because it was not exported to Europe (and thus painted by European painters). Nor was there any information about its provenance. The discovery of a large hoard of such pieces in the Great Mosque of Divriği (Map 2) in the early 1970s and the eventual exhibition and publication of many of them by the Vakıflar Museum in Istanbul, was complemented by the publication of another similar and significant group of almost unknown Anatolian pile carpets in the Berlin collections. Today, important early Anatolian pile rugs, many of them in damaged or fragmentary condition but nevertheless of great beauty, appear occasionally in the market, and serious collectors are paying high prices for them.

3. New Formats   A second "new frontier" in Anatolian pile rugs consisted for the most part of nineteenth-century pieces in formats other than the familiar *sejjadeh,* or prayer rug. These included small double-bags (Turkish *heybe*), and pile-woven pillow faces called *yastık* (literally, "cushion"), some that could be identified with traditional provenance towns, and others that could only be localized by broad geographic area. These pieces are very small (the average size of a yastik is about eighteen by thirty inches), but often not only very beautiful but very interesting in terms of their artistic pedigree. Some examples were adapted from early Turkish silk velvet cushions (Plate 31); others show in a very small space powerful medallion designs usually associated with larger carpets. Yastık rugs from Turkey are among the most favored Anatolian rugs sought by today's collectors, and fine early examples, while pricey, still appear regularly in dealer showrooms and auction catalogues.

4. Anatolian Nomadic Rugs   The final group of older Anatolian rugs in vogue among today's collectors is a group of pile weavings broadly termed Yörük. This word means "those who walk"— i.e., "nomads"—and is applied to groups of Anatolian weavings thought to have been woven by pastoral tribal groups who in Anatolia generally move between fixed summer and winter grazing areas. Most of these groups have now been forced to settle permanently in villages, as open grazing land and migration paths have been parceled up for other uses. Their traditions are rapidly disappearing, and have been the subject of intense study by anthropologists. Some of the older groups of Yörük weavings acquired particular names through their appearance in significant numbers as gifts to mosques at either end of migration pathways. Such are the rugs associated, for example, with the central Anatolian town of Şarkişla—literally, "eastern winter pasture." Another group, consisting of kilims, brocaded rugs, and pile-woven rugs made with a limited palette in which blue and red dominate, and with designs consisting of interlocking hooked forms, showed up in the marketplace of the northwest Anatolian town of Balıkesir. We now know that they were woven by a tribal group known as the Yünjü (Yüncü) (literally, "the wool people"), whose mountain pastures (yayla) are found in the hills above Balıkesir. Popularized by two circulating exhibitions from the Carnegie Museum and The Textile Museum, "Yörük" and "Flowers of the Yayla," Yörük rugs from Turkey are now actively pursued by many collectors.

CONTEMPORARY ANATOLIAN RUG-WEAVING

Contemporary Turkish rugs were until quite recently of almost no interest to collectors. The rural products tended to use unattractive aniline dyes, and the urban products of Kayseri or Hereke were, because of their lack of a distinctive local design tradition and their use of atypical techniques and materials, of little artistic or historical interest. In recent years, Hereke has become the scene of a variety of interesting weavings, including what might almost be termed small-scale "reproductions" of classical Ottoman and Safavid court carpets, some woven with knot densities up to 2,000 or more per square inch, and many with silk warp, weft, and pile.

Of more interest to most collectors, however, has been the unprecedented revival in Turkey of traditional wool dyeing, coupled with designs carefully adapted from old museum pieces. Originated in the 1970s, the movement began with a government-sponsored cooperative known by the acronym DOBAG, centered in two areas with long histories of weaving: the Yuntdağ region near Manisa in west Anatolia, and the Ayvajık region in the northwest. It was sponsored jointly by the provincial governments of these two regions and by Marmara University in Istanbul. The village women who weave for the project attach their names on a special label on the back of each rug. The colors, designs, and construction are traditional, and the entire project has been supported by anthropological and ethnographic research as well as by research in the history and chemistry of dyestuffs. In addition, the project is designed to ensure that the maximum financial gain from the creation of a carpet goes to the local weaver and her cooperative, rather than to an entrepreneur or dealer.

The success of the DOBAG project has prompted commercal imitators who often carry things several steps further. The dye traditionally used for dark brown or black in old Anatolian rugs is corrosive to wool. Over time, even though the rest of the pile on the rug may remain in excellent condition, the browns or blacks will slowly wear away, leaving in many cases only the bases of the knots. The result is a subdued dark outlining traditionally used to emphasize and separate colored forms in Anatolian weaving. The new DOBAG rugs, because their brown-black outlining is very much in evidence, sometimes disturbed the sensibilities of collectors accustomed to the corroded black. Therefore, Turkish dealers and producers of imitations of the DOBAG rugs began to employ small boys using tiny scissors to clip down *only the black knots* on their brand-new traditionally dyed rugs. This made them even closer in appearance to the antique examples so beloved of collectors. Finally, because the bright colors of true Anatolian weaving were often too strong for the taste of customers, dealers succumbed to the temptation to revert to the old dealer practice of chemically "washing" the rugs—a more appropriate term would be chemically *altering*—to subdue the traditional colors. These "new antiques" occupy a curious artistic, intellectual, and moral position in the rug world; despite their occasional appeal to those ignorant of the historical and aesthetic traditions of Anatolia, most serious collectors avoid them scrupulously. The long-term effects of chemical alteration are uncertain, but these carpets are unlikely to keep either their faded beauty or their "antique" appeal for very long.

Another offshoot of the new traditional dyeing revival has been the weaving in Anatolia of imitations of the early rugs of other areas of the Middle East, most notably the south Caucasus and northwest Persia. Because old rugs from these areas are now prohibitively expensive and hard to find, the new Turkish imitations are very attractive in the marketplace, and in some cases are visually quite uncannily similar to the works they imitate. These rugs have found special favor with collectors who prefer not to put their very expensive antique originals on the floor, and substitute instead what might be termed very attractive, well-researched "reproductions." Although expensive, such imitations are certainly nowhere near as pricey (or, in many cases, as fragile) as the antique originals that inspired them.

$\mathscr{W}$HAT ARE TRANSCAUCASIAN CARPETS?

INTRODUCTION

The mountainous area east of the Black Sea and west of the Caspian, north of Iran and Anatolia and south of the Ukraine, and now including the newly independent states of Georgia, Armenia, and Azerbaijan, is known as Transcaucasia, because it straddles two great mountain ranges named the Greater and Lesser Caucasus (Map 3). The term *Caucasian*, sometimes used to describe rugs from this area, is somewhat misleading to the novice, both because of its racial connotations, and because of the erroneous *-asian* of the last two syllables. No other rug-weaving area has so much geographical and ethnic diversity in such a small area. Sadly, few areas in the world today are experiencing more ethnic strife. From the late eleventh century onward, most of the ancient indigenous peoples of the Caucasus lived under Persian and Turkish rule, until the eventual domination of the area by the expanding Russian empire in the nineteenth century. In addition to an incredible cauldron of ethnicities and languages, Shi'ite and Sunnite Muslims are mixed with Russian Orthodox, Armenian, and Georgian Christians, while pastoral nomads mingle with peasants, villagers, and city dwellers; it is not only impossible completely to disentangle all of the artistic threads constituting the artistic heritage of Transcaucasia, but as a practical consequence rather pointless as well.

There are documents before the eleventh century linking rug-weaving with Armenian peoples, and Armenians have for centuries been involved in the carpet trade. Turkic peoples have constituted a significant proportion of the overall population of Transcaucasia since 1100, as well as constituting a sizable segment of the ruling class. But the earliest surviving Caucasian rugs, among them the so-called Dragon Carpets (Plate 32) and Kuba Carpets, are related to the Iranian weaving tradition, and are dated to the seventeenth century and later. Not surprisingly, these and other early carpets from Transcaucasia have been hotly claimed as part of the cultural heritage of various ethnic groups, but the best art-historical evidence suggests that most of them incorporate designs derived from earlier Iranian carpets of Kerman, including motifs of Chinese origin such as dragons, ducks, and antelope-like creatures known as *chi'lin*. Like their Iranian forebears, the early Transcaucasian carpets tend to be very large, with a length at least two-and-a-half times the width, and most of the elements of their designs suggest their derivation from a group of seventeenth-century Iranian commercial carpets in many different kinds of designs known collectively as "vase technique" rugs. However, virtually all carpets woven in Transcaucasia, whether old or new, used the symmetrical knot, and the older ones especially utilize many of the same dyestuffs and same range of hues as their Anatolian cousins.

This very brief overview of the background of Transcaucasian

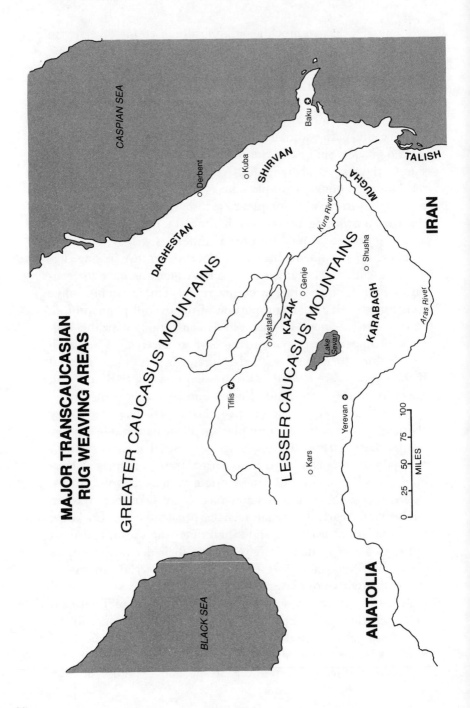

MAJOR TRANSCAUCASIAN
RUG WEAVING AREAS

weaving serves to establish several important points: Like their Anatolian cousins, which they resemble in technique, coloration, and some shared types of designs, later Caucasian carpets trace their roots back to a complex past. And because the area was overrun by both Ottomans and Safavids, Transcaucasian weaving traditions bear the impress of both cultures, mingled with the complex mixture of indigenous peoples and cultures. Beyond this, there is no easy summary way to characterize Transcaucasian carpets.

The Nineteenth-Century Rug Revival in Transcaucasia

When carpet-weaving revived in Transcaucasia in the nineteenth century, apparently encouraged as economic activity by the Russian rulers, the new production tended to be largely in small formats such as the *sejjadeh,* or prayer rug. Only rarely did these carpets attain weft dimensions (width) greater than 2 to 2½ meters, thus ignoring the market for "room sized" weaving for export to the parlors and dining rooms of the West, then dominated by the weavings of Iran.

Transcaucasian rugs share with Anatolian rugs the tendency to exhibit a very rich variety of design ancestry. The loosely woven, long-piled, and powerfully designed carpets of the south Caucasus known as *Kazaks,* for example (Plate 33), not only include numbers of weavings suggestive of the large-pattern Holbeins from Anatolia with their large octagonal medallions and "2-1-2" arrangement of forms, they also show what may be viewed as somewhat bizarre adaptations, on a huge scale, of designs from delicate silk embroideries of earlier times (Plates 34, 35). Other rugs, such as those from the areas closer to the Caspian shore, quite commonly borrow individual motifs from the earlier "dragon rugs" and "Kuba carpets."

SCHÜRMANN'S
CAUCASIAN RUG GROUPS

In the later nineteenth century, around the same time that merchants from Tabriz began the revival of carpet-weaving in Iran, certain areas of Transcaucasia saw a dramatic increase in rug production. Rugs of this period have been divided into categories in various ways; Ulrich Schürmann, the German author, mapped out ten major groupings and dozens of subgroups, and the names he published in the 1960s now constitute the basic nomenclature of Transcaucasian rugs. More recently, authors not comfortable with Schürmann's place-names have fallen back on broader categories. These are:

1. Rugs of the southwest Caucasus (including Schürmann's **Kazak, Karabagh,** and **Genje** groups), which tend to be loose in weave, long in pile, and have in most cases large-scale geometric designs, with shiny wool and brilliant hues. Of these, the best-known are the **Kazak** rugs, which usually have a red-dyed weft, often with four or six shots of weft between each row of knots; a coarse weave; a flat, usually red or blue selvedge; and despite all this, a substantial "handle." These carpets come in a wide range of designs, among them the Karachov, with its octagonal Holbein medallion; the Borjaly, with its pattern of interlocking hooks; and the Star and Pinwheel Kazaks (Plate 8), with designs derived from earlier embroideries. The **Karabagh** group is harder to define; some examples are strikingly similar to Kazaks, but often with a much flabbier "handle" and with buff-colored or undyed white weft, and a proclivity for a darker purply red color thought to come from insect dye and for large areas of pile dyed in corrosive dark brown. The **Genje** group is the finest in weave, often exhibits a multicolored selvedge (sometimes red and blue), and often exhibits the *boteh* motif—sometimes referred to as the "paisley" design— and/or a design of diagonal stripes.

2. Rugs of the east Caucasus (including Schürmann's **Shirvan,**

Kuba, and **Baku** groups) tend as a group to be narrower than southwest Caucasus rugs and finer in weave, with precise and often repetitive designs. These as a group are the most direct descendants of the earlier "classical" Transcaucasian rugs of the seventeenth century, the Dragon and Kuba carpets. There are many formulas used to distinguish among the subgroups, and few authors are in complete agreement. In general, rugs of the **Shirvan** group are of medium knot density, are often woven in long formats (around 3½ by 8½ feet). They often have a three-ply warp using yarns of both brown and white wool (the warp, after all, is the most convenient place to hide the undesirable brown wool), and the selvedge is often white.

The **Kuba** group, similar in knot density to the Shirvan group, may be more finely knotted. It often has a blue selvedge and blue brocading on the edges and ends, if these have survived intact and without restoration, and often shows a slight depression of alternate warps. **Baku** rugs, as conventionally defined, are often among the largest of later Transcaucasian weavings, and many examples show design elements taken from contemporary rugs of the Kurdish areas of Iran to the south.

3. Rugs of the north Caucasus (the area known as **Daghestan** ("mountain-land") are among the finest in weave, and are supposedly identifiable by a two-level warp giving them a stiffer "handle" (Plate 36). The best-known of the many design types is a characteristic prayer-rug design with a perfunctory "arch" at the top. However, this popular design was also borrowed by the weavers of the eastern Caucasus. Other north Caucasus rugs have been associated with Turkic tribal groups, among them the **Lesghi** and the **Chechen,** the latter sometimes called "Chi-chi" in the trade.

4. A group of tribal rugs from the southeast Caucasus (Schürmann's **Mughan** and **Talish** rugs, and some weavings of Shah Sevan nomads who inhabit parts of Transcaucasia, Turkey, and Iran). These are woven in a variety of designs, most with clear ties to earlier Iranian, Transcaucasian, and

Anatolian traditions. Most of these are long and narrow rugs of medium knot density that often have colors and wool as brilliant and lustrous as the Kazak and Genje examples. The best-known type of so-called **Mughan** design (Plate 37) is closely akin to the Anatolian Memling rugs, while the archetypal **Talish** often exhibits a single-color field, usually blue, surrounded by a characteristic border.

FLAT-WOVEN RUGS FROM TRANSCAUCASIA

Flat-woven rugs from Transcaucasia have also been for some time very attractive acquisitions for Western collectors. The exceptions are the large, "room sized" rugs in sumak brocading technique, often with aniline dyes, that represented in the decade before World War I an attempted challenge to Iranian weavers in a cheaper, flat-woven product. The far more interesting small sumak pieces that used to be attributed to parts of the Caucasus are now chiefly recognized as products of the Shah Sevan, a Turkic nomadic group whose grazing grounds were found primarily in extreme north Iran. (This will be discussed in more detail in the next section of this book.) Transcaucasian kilims made before the aniline blight are often quite splendid; some types follow the old east Caucasus practice of drawing on Iranian models such as the Kuba kilims, with their designs of large lotus palmettes surrounded by a simple border. The majority of kilims from this area are without vertical borders and exhibit a variety of designs in a format with lateral stripes, often incorporating brocading as well as the slit-tapestry technique. They sometimes use brilliant white cotton wefts in their white areas for additional visual effect.

REVISIONIST SCHOLARSHIP

More recent research, especially that undertaken by the American Richard Wright using Russian economic records from the late nineteenth century, has demythologized much of Caucasian weaving, suggesting that these rugs so beloved of Western collectors were woven almost entirely by individuals of Turkic origin working for export-oriented entrepreneurs. It has also been suggested that the many characteristic nineteenth-century Transcaucasian carpet designs, rather than having evolved slowly over time, may represent an explosion of market-oriented invention.

Schürmann's groupings described above have also been redefined in part by Latif Kerimov, a rug specialist from Azerbaijan. The existence of sizable numbers of carpets from all over the Transcaucasus, but especially from the Kazak and Karabagh areas in the south, with inscriptions in the Armenian alphabet, has led to suggestions that some of the weavers of these rugs may have been Armenian. And most recently, entirely new categories of Transcaucasian weaving—such as the Avar group, with its predominately red and blue palette—have been set forth in publications.

COLLECTING TRANSCAUCASIAN RUGS

Needless to say, despite the academic controversies in the field, the best examples of Transcaucasian carpets remain highly desirable. The Caucasian carpet mania of the late sixties appears to have calmed down a bit, except for certain rugs of the Kazak group, most notably the aptly named Star Kazak group (Plate 8), with its designs of geometric stars on a white ground. Examples of this style have sometimes obtained auction prices far higher than those paid for great "classical" carpets of the sixteenth and seventeenth centuries.

In the fifties and sixties, the American collector tempted by the beauties of Transcaucasian carpet-weaving lived in paradise, for the great world source for these works of art was the northeastern United States. Thousands of small "scatter rugs"—small rugs used as accents on floors, in contrast to the larger "room sized" formats—from Transcaucasia had flooded into the Middle Atlantic and especially the New England states before World

War I. Many of these rugs were sold by the pioneering first generation of Armenian-American rug dealers, and became common interior furnishings, often appearing in New England estate auctions. After the publication of the first edition of Schürmann's book in 1961, and especially after the appearance of an international edition with parallel English and German texts, American auction prices began to rise. Still, even in the late 1960s, examples of many of the finest Transcaucasian weavings were still obtainable for a few hundred dollars.

The collector seriously interested in these weavings usually starts by purchasing a copy of Schürmann (see the bibliography, chapter 12; the English edition periodically appears in new, ever more expensive editions). Unfortunately, many collectors disregard Schürmann's useful warning at the outset that it is structure, rather than design, that is the most important determinant of provenance in Transcaucasian carpets. Intelligent collecting practice for these rugs is quite similar to that for their Anatolian cousins. In searching for fine old examples, the most important factor affecting the collector's judgment should be good color: Many Caucasian rugs of otherwise impeccable coloring will exhibit a bit of strident aniline orange or runny aniline pink, and thousands more were subjected to color-altering washes that left them with faded indigo blue and assorted obnoxious varieties of near-beige (Plate 9). A very beautifully woven group of rugs in impeccably "authentic" designs was produced after the Bolshevik revolution, apparently as part of a government program to earn foreign exchange. These so-called NEP (after Lenin's New Economic Policy) rugs can sometimes be identified by very uniform chromium-dyed pile, unmarked by the traditional subtle abrash, and by a rather crisp, often almost metallic rigidity in their designs.

Navigating between the Scylla of schlock and the Charybdis of the NEP can in itself be a daunting task; trying to pick outstanding examples from the considerable number of very respectable "authentic" Caucasian rugs still available can be even more difficult at first. Here, as in all collecting, one's best tactic is continually to compare examples in the same design and technical grouping. Fortunately, given the large number of exhibitions that have featured these rugs, and the large number of Transcaucasian rugs featured in color advertisements in *Hali* (the international magazine devoted primarily to Oriental rugs) and other glossy magazines, there is a wealth of published material of great value for comparative looking. After good color, good design is the second imperative, closely followed by reasonably good condition. "Reasonably good" means that the carpet does not exhibit sizable areas of wear that have come close to obliterating the design. Finely woven Caucasus rugs in particular, because they often have white weft and warp, are vulnerable to the practice of "painting" with dyes or with felt-tip markers in worn areas. In the southwest Caucasus carpets, where long, lustrous pile in brilliant colors is often by far the most important part of a carpet's visual appeal, overall condition of pile is even more important. Remember, however, that only rarely does a respectably old carpet avoid developing a few areas of patchy wear. And while fragmentary or raggedy Anatolian rugs, especially older kilims, have become more and more respectable among collectors, the same is not true of their Transcaucasian cousins. It is important to remember that the overwhelming majority of desirable, collectible carpets from Transcaucasia were woven in a very brief period—the few decades between 1880 and World War I—and thus, except in rare cases, exceptional age is *not* a major factor in the acquisition of these weavings, nor should it be.

Likewise, in collecting Caucasus rugs, the pedigree of the nineteenth-century rug, the closeness of its artistic relation to its historical forebears, is not in most cases a major factor. Because so many of the designs are market-oriented inventions rather than incrementally evolved survivors, there is a compensating freshness, variety, and originality to be found in many of these carpets. Even the most traditional designs, such as those found in the so-called Mughan and Kazak groups, are likely to be extensively embellished by the weaver, who through custom often felt free to insert into her weavings a plethora of images from daily life. These might include animal and human forms, depictions of objects (among them various rug-weaving implements such as scissors and comb hammers—and vast numbers of inscriptions (more often than not illegible) and dates (more often than not unreliable.)

With the exception of the NEP rugs already mentioned, there has been little significant modern rug-weaving from Transcaucasia in the aftermath of Sovietization. Certain commercial manufactories were encouraged, especially in what are now the republics of Armenia and Azerbaijan, but in general their rugs are only rarely seen in the West, and of little interest to collectors. On the other hand, the fall of the Soviet Union has led to a flood of older rugs from Transcaucasia reaching the West, especially via the rug markets of Turkey. For example, until 1991 this writer had laid eyes on only two kilims of the so-called Avar type; in a few weeks in the summer of 1991, without looking very hard, I saw almost two dozen examples in collections and dealer showrooms in Turkey. The result: Prices of older Transcaucasian pieces have actually fallen a bit in recent years, especially in Turkey, their major outlet to the West. Therefore, they are once again of great interest to the novice collector.

With the new influx of old pieces—including previously unpublished and unstudied types—appearing in the West in the early 1990s, rugs from Transcaucasia promise to be a continuing source of interest to collectors and will doubtless also continue to provoke a great deal of lively and stimulating rug literature.

CHAPTER 5

*W*HAT ARE IRANIAN CARPETS?

INTRODUCTION

In the popular imagination, the terms *Oriental carpet* and *Persian carpet* are virtually synonymous, and for good reason. The great Persian carpets of the classical age of the sixteenth and seventeenth centuries C.E., commissioned by the Safavid court for royal use or woven as royal gifts, rank among the greatest artistic accomplishments of Persian art in particular, and of Islamic art in general. Rarer in the West than the more familiar carpets from Anatolia, the classical carpets of the Iranian tradition appear less frequently in European paintings. The fineness of their weave, the originality and elegant perfection of their curvilinear designs, their wide palette of colors, and their often quite vast size have impressed later generations of rug weavers, as well as European and American collectors, for centuries. The old Persian carpets were among the first to enter European museum collections in the nineteenth century. Although until recently it was difficult to trace the history of Persian weaving back to before the year 1500, the tradition belongs to a culture whose lineage goes back two-and-a-half millennia to the time of such kings as Cyrus the Great and Xerxes, great rivals of classical Greece in its days of glory.

For our purposes, *Iran* is a geographical term (Map 4), tra-ditionally encompassing not only the modern state of that name in the Middle East, but also parts of what are today Afghanistan and the Üzbek republic to the east and northeast. The dominant ethnic group in Iran today is the Persians, who speak an Indo-European language called Farsi that is akin to English, French, and German. For the most part, the Persians belong to a Shi'ite branch of Islam known as Imami, or "Twelver," Shi'ism, and today's Persians (their religious rulers notwithstanding) often view themselves as the heirs of a cultural tradition stretching back into pre-Islamic times. But Iran has significant ethnic mi-norities as well, many of them active in rug-weaving: The largest of these groups is the Azeris, Turkish-speaking Shi'ites who in-habit the large area of northwest Iran known as Azerbaijan, and who are closely akin in culture and language to their northern neighbors across the border of what used to be the Soviet Union. Also here in Azerbaijan is a Turkic nomadic people known as the Shah Sevan—literally, "those who love the king"—prolific weavers famous for their small brocaded rugs in sumak technique. In the west, and in a few other pockets around the country, are the Kurds, also an Indo-European people of great antiquity. They are mostly settled villagers and townspeople who are related to the Kurds of Iraq, Syria, and Turkey. West Iran is also the homeland of the largest and formerly the most powerful of Iranian seminomadic tribes, the Bakhtiyari. In the southwest, centered in winter around the cities of Shiraz and Kerman, are a number of nomadic or seminomadic rug-weaving tribal groups, including the Turkic Qashqa'i and Afshar.

In northeast Iran—ancient Khorasan—are the nomadic Bal-uch, another Indo-European tribal group, branches of which are

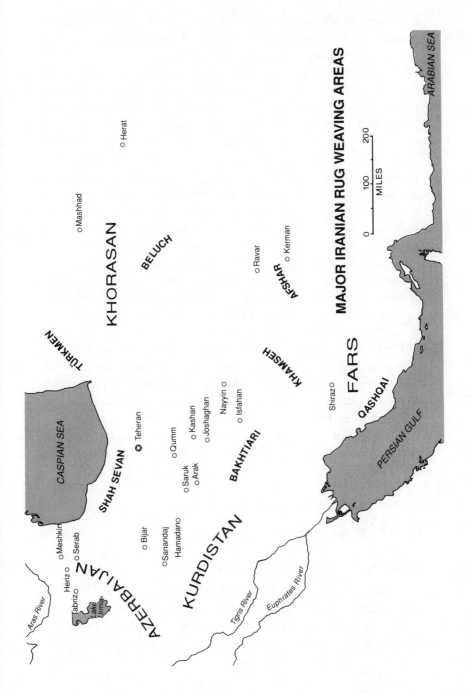

MAJOR IRANIAN RUG WEAVING AREAS

also found in Afghanistan and Pakistan. And in the north of Iran are also found elements of the central Asian Türkmen tribes to be discussed in the next section of this book.

As mentioned, there is often a profound difference between rugs woven in cities under the aegis of export-oriented entrepreneurs and rugs woven in villages and nomadic encampments primarily for the use of the weavers and their families. The latter group is woven in the same way as the village and nomadic weaving we have encountered in Anatolia and Transcaucasia. The commercial weaving of the cities, however, has a more complex division of labor. The weavers working in the urban carpet manufactories are commonly young boys, whose low wage requirements and quick fingers are well suited to the finely knotted technique. The instructions are either the familiar graph-paper cartoon, which in the case of a carpet covered with repetitive patterns could be fairly small, or a device known as a *talim,* which presents the knotting schema in a form of shorthand notation, and which can be read aloud or chanted to several weavers who produce identical carpets side by side in an urban workshop.

Because the vast range of Iranian carpets of interest to collectors encompasses both urban and traditional weavings, we will discuss them under separate headings, remembering that in rug weaving, artistic cross-fertilization is never absent from any tradition for long. Our brief summary discussion of the very complex Iranian urban weaving tradition begins in Turkish-speaking northwest Iran, with its political and economic capital in the city of Tabriz.

IRANIAN CITY RUGS

A. RUGS OF NORTHWEST IRAN

1. Tabriz It was Tabrizi merchants who in the mid- to late nineteenth century helped to bring about the great modern revival of Iranian carpet weaving. Tabriz city weaving of the late nineteenth and early twentieth centuries consists largely of finely woven carpets that in many ways are typical of high-quality Iranian city weaving (Plate 38). Often made in large, "room-sized" formats, Tabriz rugs were woven in a variety of designs, including adaptations of the Ardebil Carpet and other classical Iranian carpets. Because of their large size and scale, they are not normally the object of collector interest. Smaller-format Tabriz rugs, however, are a different story. They are finely woven, with a typical density of around 250 knots in a square inch, using a wool pile and a characteristic Iranian multi-ply cotton warp on two levels, usually with every other warp almost invisible on the back, and a cotton weft. Designs are intricate and curvilinear; one of the most common patterns is the so-called *herati* pattern (Plate 39), a vegetal network of curving leaves, sometimes popularly called "fish" by rug dealers, together with stylized lotus palmettes and rosettes. Medallions in various shapes are common in small and large Tabriz weaving. *Sejjadeh* rugs inspired by Turkish examples from Gördes, sometimes executed entirely of silk, were at one time popular with collectors. The finest of the Tabriz silk rugs in terms of construction—500 kpsi (knots per square inch) or higher—were for some reason called "Heriz silks" on the marketplace. The reason for their attractiveness to collectors, apart from their fineness, has somehow completely escaped this writer, since their designs are often either derivative or downright bizarre, and their colors tend to be extremely dull.

In Tabriz rugs the corner resolutions of major and minor borders tend to be arbitrary, but not obtrusively so. In other words, the border adjustments are usually left to the skilled weaver rather than being woven from detailed instructions in cartoon or *talim* form. The pile wool is often hard and dry to the touch, and a light chemical wash was often used to soften the colors, leaving a characteristic light reddish brown with little luster. Sometimes designs were shared among major urban rug-weaving centers in Iran, but Tabriz rugs are generally fairly easy for the collector to identify. They remain the only major group of finely woven, cotton-warped city rugs from Iran executed with a symmetrical knot, but because of the two-level warp and the fineness of the weave, the only practical way to observe this feature is to "deconstruct" part of the rug (definitely *not* recommended!) or to find a hole, stripped edge, or end where the knot structure may be observed.

2. Heriz District   To the north of Tabriz, centered around the city of Heriz, a much different kind of carpet was produced. It utilized a much coarser weave and partook of a different artistic tradition in which the geometric power of designs similar to those of Transcaucasia to the north was much in evidence. The older examples, which tend to be quite large and woven on a wool foundation with a density of around 100 kpsi, are sometimes called "Serab" or "Serabi" on the market. Today they are among the most highly sought-after and frequently imitated of all Iranian rugs, because of the boldness and geometric nature of their designs and their marvelous colors and robust construction (Plate 10). Long and narrow wool-warped rugs from this area, which are often woven with a plain light-brown outer border, used to be called "camel-hair runners" in the trade. The undyed brown knots are, however, almost always created from sheep wool. Similar weavings, with a different but also bold and craggy repertoire of designs—and often a much greater length in comparison to their width—are termed "Bakhshaish." Later examples, with a cotton foundation, but also with attractive large-scale geometric medallion or patterned designs, are simply called "Heriz," or, if particularly coarse (around 50 kpsi), "Gorevan." All of these rugs from Azerbaijan are tied with a symmetrical knot, and they represent one of the few instances in Iranian city rugs where a bold and geometric style, itself stemming from the geometry of the loom, is directly applied to the format of the large, room-sized carpet, and in designs that are almost always stylized descendants of the great curvilinear patterns of the classical age of the sixteenth and seventeenth centuries.

B. IRANIAN KURDISH WEAVING

1. Hamadan   South of Azerbaijan is the part of Iran where Kurds make up a significant part of the population. Three cities in this area in particular are associated with rug-weaving. The rugs of Hamadan, the most numerous, are of little interest to collectors; they constitute the bottom rung on the ladder of rug status in Iran, although some individual examples may be of better quality. Hamadan rugs are woven in a variety of patterns—in the main, derived from those of other weaving areas—and they tend to be coarse and wear poorly. Hamadans are woven with loosely plied cotton warps and wefts, and are often single-wefted, and thus identifiable by the appearance of alternating "dashes" of white cotton warp on the back.

2. Sehna By contrast, the rugs associated with the districts around the cities of Sanandaj (Sehna) and Bijar are highly sought after by collectors. They are as different as they can be; the thin, finely knotted, short-piled, supple Sehna rugs, with their single cotton wefts and cotton or multicolored silk warps, are among the finest and most delicate to come from Iran (Plate 39). Woven with crisp and detailed designs, almost always incorporating areas of herati pattern, Sehna rugs tend to be small. In addition to various types of carpets, they occasionally appear in the saddle rug and double-bag formats, and when an old Sehna rug has managed to avoid the dulling chemical wash that unfortunately was common treatment for the rugs of this area, the colors are quite marvelous. Although some rug authors persist in using the terms *Gördes* and *Sehna* for the symmetrical and asymmetrical knots, it is worth remembering that Sehna rugs are always woven with the "Gördes"—that is to say, the symmetrical—knot, a good reason for ignoring these archaic and confusing terms.

Collectors of Iranian rugs also know the Sehna area for its kilims; these seem an almost total contradiction of the technique itself, in their highly detailed and delicate designs. When held up to the light, a Sehna kilim's myriads of slits light up like the Milky Way, and one must marvel at how the gifted weavers of these interesting and complex carpets in effect triumphed over the limitations of the slit-tapestry technique in creating what are frequently masterpieces.

3. Bijar   If the Sehna rug is the delicate coloratura soprano of the Kurdish weaving opera, then the Bijar is the brawny basso profundo. The older Bijars, woven up to around 1900, appear in many different designs, of which a huge red and white arabesque on a blue-black ground is perhaps the most famous (Plate 40). Large Bijars were also frequently woven in medallion designs. The range of formats is equally impressive, from small saddlebags and medium-sized "sampler rugs," or *vagireh,* much in demand among collectors, to gigantic room-sized carpets which are among the most expensive and sought after of all large Iranian rugs. Examples with dated inscriptions naming the master weaver are sometimes found in examples from the late nineteenth century.

The oldest and best of these rugs are woven on strong woolen warps that are forced into two levels, with only one visible from the back. The wefts are packed down on each row of knots by a pair of tools—a beating comb often serving as an anvil, which is then hit with a mallet to pack the knots very tightly. As a result, a great old Bijar is about as supple as a sheet of marine plywood, and should *never* be folded, but only rolled. The gesture of turning over a corner of a rug with the toe of one's shoe is of varying utility, but the response of a heavy, stiff Bijar to one's well-shod foot is unique. Aptly dubbed the "iron rugs of Persia," Bijars have their devotees in the person of specialist collectors, for whom, next to these muscle men of the rug world, all other rugs are weak and effete. A corollary to the great strength of Bijars, however (and a warning as well): Because one can force a needle through a Bijar only with great difficulty, these rugs, once torn or worn, are extremely difficult if not virtually impossible to repair well.

C. ARAK DISTRICT

To the east of the Kurdish area of Iran lies the Arak district, probably the most prolific area in the rug-weaving world by the year 1900. There are many names associated with this district, from the finely woven Saruk (sometimes spelled Sarouk out of deference to the French, for whom it makes a difference), the group of rugs named after the plain of Feraghan (often spelled

Ferahan), to the lowly, uncollectible Lilahan, with its coarse weave and chemically altered colors. Many of the weavers from the various ethnic groups living in the Arak area labored for piecework wages for companies controlled by Tabrizi or European entrepreneurs, and the greater part of the output was in the form of large, room-sized carpets destined in the main for Europe and North America. However, rugs woven in smaller formats in the techniques and designs associated with the names Saruk and Feraghan are among the most highly prized Iranian rugs for collectors. As with the Bijars and Sehnas woven by Kurds to the west, the two Arak groups are very unlike each other in design and technique.

1. Saruk   The older Saruk rugs from before the 1930s are on the whole quite finely woven with a short pile, and very carefully planned as to corner articulation. Many were made with medallion designs in a variety of sizes and formats that include small carpets, and even an occasional double bag, saddle rug, or *sejjadeh*. Old Saruk rugs share with some of the urban weavings of Kashan a kind of drawing in which a dark indigo blue outline defines most of the forms, and pinkish red and indigo predominate in the palette. While fine, they are not particularly supple, as their cotton warps are on two levels and their often blue-dyed wefts are packed tight. Later rugs woven in the 1930s, also termed Saruk on the market and also finely woven, have a much longer, plushy pile and were usually first bleached and then painted with mulberry red and blue before being sold.

2. Feraghan   The rugs commonly called Feraghan or Ferahan encompass a considerable range of quality as measured by fineness of wool and by knot density. Around 1900, huge, fairly coarsely woven room-sized Feraghan carpets were produced in enormous numbers, together with matching "runners," in identical and often boring herati patterns, usually on a blue ground. Indeed, for some Iranians, the herati pattern is called instead the "Feraghan design." For collectors, it is the small, finely woven Feraghan carpets that create the greatest interest; these at their best can be so sensational that even the most hardened Kazak afficionado or Türkmen fanatic cannot resist their charms (Plate 11). The range of designs is extensive, from traditional medallions and overall patterns to the elaborate swaying bunches of flowers called in Iran the *zil-e sultan* pattern. The designers apparently had a good deal of freedom to use original ideas, and the colors can be as fresh as a garden of spring flowers. Collected with passion for a long time both in Iran and the West, the best small Feraghan rugs are rare and expensive.

D. OTHER CITY WEAVING

Among the other city rugs of the Iranian rug revival that are of interest to collectors are the products of Mashhad (the main city of the northeastern district of Khorasan), Joshaghan and Kashan (cities in central Iran with a long history of weaving), and Kerman, for centuries a major rug-weaving center in south Iran. Rug weaving in the two last-named towns goes back to the classical period: The name of the designer of the Ardebil Carpet—Maqsud of Kashan—is woven into the carpet itself, while Kerman was especially famous in the seventeenth century for its carpets woven in the so-called vase technique. Among the carpets from the later nineteenth and early twentieth centuries woven in each of these towns are examples that appeal to today's collector.

1. Kashan   Kashan rugs, among the finest in weave of the older Iranian rugs, show a limited palette of subdued colors quite similar to that of the best Saruk weavings, together with a variety of sizes from large, room-sized examples to smaller carpets around six by four feet. Designs vary from the traditional medallion form (Plate 41) to so-called picture rugs that show illustrations of characters and episodes from Persian narrative poems. The pricey Kashan category comprises a number of subgroups, including the so-called *mohtashem Kashan* (*mohtashem* means "great" or "important") with dark blue outlining, and the even more exotic "Manchester Kashan"—the Manchester in question being the large industrial city in the English Midlands whose factories allegedly produced the worsted pile wool and the cotton warp used in such weavings. Collectors who prize Kashan rugs generally do so because of the precision and fineness of the weave and the intricacy of the designs, with their carefully turned corners and occasional inclusion of birds or animals among the floral ornament. Knowledgeable collectors also recognize Kashan rugs by certain distinctive ornaments, such as a particular kind of reciprocal guard border used almost exclusively by Kashan designers.

2. Kerman   City rugs of Kerman, one of the most abundant sources of Iranian carpets, are primarily of large format. The older "Laver Kerman" rugs associated with the nearby town of Raver were once used as highly prestigious floor coverings in houses of the wealthy in Europe and North America. However, today's collector interest in Kerman rugs is confined in the main to a few finely woven rugs in small formats. Among these are a small group of "superfine" Kermans, with up to 800–900 kpsi. Also of interest are the "picture rugs" of Kerman that were woven in many sizes (Plate 42). Some of these take their subjects from classical Persian literature, some show views of monuments in Persian cities, and others show figures as diverse as George Washington, Socrates, and Louis XIV of France standing around talking to each other in a kind of dry (in all senses) cocktail party. Kerman rugs from the late nineteenth and early twentieth centuries frequently bear inscriptions mentioning the weaving workshop; these generally appear in a cartouche at the top end of the rug, and include such well-known names as 'Ali of Kerman, and the foreign-owned firm of Castelli.

E. CONTEMPORARY IRANIAN WEAVING
When the Western taste for Iranian floor rugs gave way between the World Wars to a predilection for a new product—the broadloom carpet produced in Western factories, with its option for wall-to-wall installation—the Oriental carpet companies attempted to strike back. From the Arak district came the washed and painted Saruk, a thick, heavy, plushy carpet whose original colors were removed chemically and replaced by "painting" with characteristic mulberry pink and dark blue dyes. From Kerman came even thicker and plushier rugs in pale, powder-puff pastel

colors with very broad, large-scale designs. For a price, they could even be handwoven to fit one's living room, wall to wall, with borders following the contours of one's fireplace or bay window. As interesting as these handwoven rugs may be from an economic or even a sociological point of view, however, they have as yet limited appeal for collectors. Of much greater interest are some of the new types of city rugs produced in Iran after World War II, especially the extraordinary weavings of Nayyin, Qumm, and Isfahan.

Muhammad Reza Pahlavi, the shah of Iran until his fall in the revolution of 1978, was interested in reviving the symbols of past Iranian royal glory. During his reign in the 1950s, certain ateliers in Iran, such as the Serafian firm in Isfahan, began to produce extremely finely woven carpets using very accurate re-productions and "authentic" paraphrases of classical Iranian weaving of the sixteenth century. The Isfahan and Nayyin (some-times spelled Nain, but never rhyming with "rain," "Spain," or "plain") products are sometimes very difficult to tell from one another. Commonly woven with a density of up to 900 kpsi, and even in some cases considerably finer, these "blue chip" carpets are among the most expensive contemporary rugs in the world. They are also among the few present-day Iranian weavings that are seriously collected both inside and outside of Iran (Plate 43). Together with the only slightly less fine rugs of Qumm, which sometimes include areas of silk in the pile, they constitute the highest technical level of commercial rug production attained in Iran in modern times. While some may find their designs and coloration a bit cold and stereotypical, there is no question that from the point of view of sheer technical achievement, they are often breathtaking.

The rug-weaving situation in Iran today is complex. A Western embargo against Iranian products has not significantly raised prices in Europe and America, because dealers had large stock-piles, and demand for contemporary city weaving fell off. Indeed, as Iranian students enrolled in American universities rushed to sell the rugs they had brought along as security for a rainy day, prices of some Iranian pieces actually dropped for a while. At the same time, governmental policies oppressing the traditionally independent tribal groups drastically affected the production of carpets by certain tribes. Today, the Iranian government has embarked on a new policy of promoting contemporary weaving, in part to gain sorely needed foreign exchange. As part of this promotion effort, rug fairs and scholarly symposia geared to appeal to foreign visitors are beginning once again to attract buyers to Iran.

NOMADIC RUGS FROM IRAN

A. TRIBAL RUGS OF FARS AND KERMAN

Twenty years ago, the very limited knowledge that most collectors had about Iranian nomadic rugs could be summed up in a single word: Shiraz. The old city of Shiraz, situated in the province of Fars, the heart of ancient Persia, was a major market town where the carpets woven by the tribal artists of the Qashqa'i, the Khamseh—and, to a lesser extent, the Afshar from the southeast and the Lur and Bakhtiyari from the northwest—found their way to the world marketplace. Over the last quarter-century, no area of collecting has developed more rapidly or has revealed more beautiful new types of rugs to the collecting mainstream than the area of nomadic rugs from Iran. The subject is a wide and complex one, covered in a number of recent books and catalogues listed in chapter 12 that treat not only the south and west Persian nomads just mentioned, but also the Baluch of the east; nomadic Kurds, Arabs, and Türkmen of the north; and the Shah Sevan of the northwest.

Our map gives general information on the traditional range of some of the most important of these tribal groups. Their weavings vary from highly sophisticated larger carpets much influenced by the city rugs of Iran, such as certain Qashqa'i carpets evidently woven for high tribal officials, to small functional pieces associated with nomadic life, such as the bottle-shaped salt bags or mixed-technique double flour bags. These flour bags are designed to be carried over the back of a horse or mule, and are woven in brocaded technique except for thick pile in corners and other areas subject to greater wear (Plate 44). Often south Iranian tribal pieces will show the effects of intermarriage and settlement in villages; among rugs woven by the Turkic Qashqa'i or Afshar, it is not uncommon to find, in the middle of a Persianized floral field, strongly emblematic designs such as the Memling motif, thought to be tribal symbols from the Turkic past.

While the mainly commercial city rugs of Iran, with their detailed, curvilinear designs and generally subdued colors, are markedly different in aesthetic from the traditional geometric designs and bold colors of Anatolia and the Caucasus, the nomadic rugs of Iran have a good deal in common with the weaving traditions to the west and north. For example, some kilims woven by Qashqa'i nomads in south Iran (where they are called *gelim)* bear an astonishing resemblance to kilims woven in the Shirvan area of the Caucasus. The older tribal rugs of Iran tend to use the traditional bold colors largely obtainable from local plant materials, although the aniline blight did affect parts of Iran, and industrial dyes are in common use today. And the older nomadic pieces, true to their heritage, are for the most part woven entirely of lustrous wool.

B. SHAH SEVAN RUGS

The Turkic Shah Sevan nomads of Iran, whose range in earlier times crossed what became the Turkish and Soviet borders, wove small-format pieces in sumak-brocaded technique. Because of their bold traditional designs and Turkic tribal motifs, these carpets were formerly attributed to Transcaucasia. Highly valued by collectors are the small double bags known as *khorjin* (or, in Turkey, *heybe)* that carry on the two front decorated panels designs of astonishing power and beauty, usually in a space around eighteen inches square (Plate 12). Such small bags were frequently cut up by dealers and the two faces sold separately. Such is their self-contained artistry that they command very high prices even when taken from their functional context. Even more subject to being dismantled were the larger bedding bags or "box bags" of the Shah Sevan. These flexible fabric "steamer trunks" consist of two long side panels in sumak-brocaded technique, woven in one piece on the loom, separated by a striped, tapestry-woven bottom and two small, square end pieces that are sewn on. Often decorated with designs of stylized animal forms in brilliant colors, these large functional pieces, intact or in parts, are again a major focus for today's collectors.

C. BELUCH NOMADIC RUGS

The rugs we call Beluch used to occupy a status among Iranian nomadic pieces similar to that of Hamadan rugs among city carpets. I remember in 1968 calling a country auctioneer to ask if he had any rugs in an upcoming sale. "No rugs," he replied, "just a couple of Beluch pieces." And it is true that some of these rugs, woven with very little white in their designs and using a dark palette of red, blue, and brown, looked very unimpressive after having been beaten to death under generations of barnyard boots in the "mud rooms" of New England farmhouses. In addition, Beluch rugs show a sometimes alarming tendency to appropriate designs from anywhere and everywhere; this fact often annoyed the "nomadic purists" among collectors, whose almost religious faith in a pre-Adamite origin for nomadic rug motifs strongly influenced the collecting ethos twenty years ago. In fact, like the little girl in the nursery rhyme, when Beluch rugs are good, "they are very, very good, and when they are bad, they are horrid." We now recognize that Beluch rugs at their best— both small-format bags and small carpets—can be of exceptional beauty, with their subtle, glowing colors and incredibly soft wool, often accented with a few motifs in contrasting white (Plate 13). Those courageous collectors who, back in the late sixties, defied popular wisdom and recognized the inherent beauty of Beluch pieces, deserve special applause, for their faith in beauty has triumphed over intellectual fads in the marketplace.

The world of nomadic weaving in Iran is vast, and we have barely touched the surface. Despite problems arising from politics in Iran since the revolution of 1978, fine nomadic pieces, now quite expensive when compared to their bargain prices of yesteryear, regularly appear on the market, often with very good provenance information. The amazingly high price of small Shah Sevan khorjin panels, however, has brought about imitations that are more than a sincere form of flattery. It appears that copies of these small brocaded pieces, made from old wool obtained by unraveling old kilims, are being artfully woven in the Mashhad area and passed off in the market as originals. The smart collector remembers three things: (1) *Stop* before you take the plunge, and do an orderly assessment of the rug you are thinking of buying, including a close look at its physical attributes of technique and condition; (2) *look* at as many pieces as you can, and compare them; and (3) *listen* to your fellow collectors and knowledgeable dealers.

$\mathscr{W}$HAT ARE TÜRKMEN CARPETS?

INTRODUCTION

The fourth and last major area of collecting to be discussed here is broadly termed central Asia—the lands to the north and east of Iran that today constitute the new Turkish-speaking countries of Türkmenia (Türkmenistan), Üzbekistan, Kazakhstan, and Kyrgyzstan and the new Persian-speaking country of Tajikistan, together with the Turkish-speaking Uighur areas of western China and parts of northern Afghanistan. Although there is some city carpet weaving in central Asia, especially in some of the great oasis cities of western China, interest of collectors has focused on nomadic rugs, especially on those woven by the Türkmen (often called Turkoman) tribes of western central Asia (Map 5), centered in the new Republic of Türkmenia, but also found in Iran, Afghanistan, and Üzbekistan. These pastoral nomads, who lived in domical portable dwellings made out of lashed poles covered with large slabs of felt, usually known as *yurts*, produced an as-

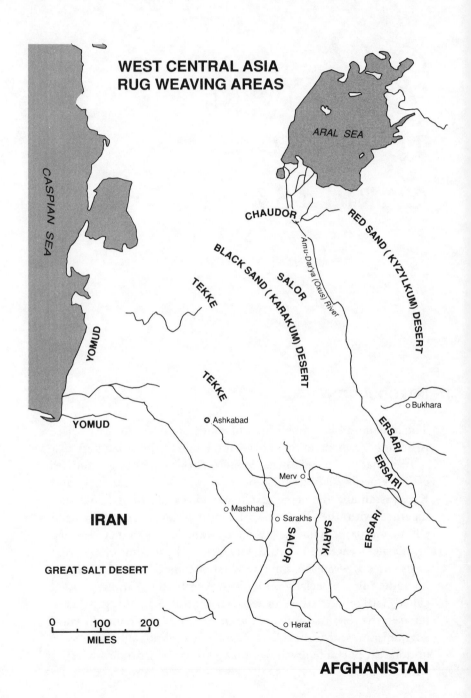

tonishing variety of rugs, little known or collected in the West until the present century.

One of the most exciting things about collecting Türkmen carpets is the abundance of genres, each one adapted to specific use in the nomadic encampment. The long, narrow tent bands were used to hold together the slabs of felt that covered the frame yurt (Illus. 21I). The *ensi* or door rug (Illus. 21A) served as the actual door of the tent. Bags, including the *chuval* (Illus. 21B), the *mafrash* (Illus. 21C), and the small *torba* (Illus. 21D), were adapted to specific uses, as were the *ok-bash* (literally, "arrowhead," Illus. 21F) used to hold spindles or tent stakes, and the *bohcha* (literally, "wrapper"). The *bohcha* is a rug woven with tapestry weave in the middle and pile on the four corners, which were then turned in as flaps and stitched together to make an envelope that varied in size; it was used to hold everything from flat bread to jewelry. Main carpets (Plate 45) were woven to cover tent floors. For special occasions, trappings such as the rectangular *kejebe* (Illus. 21L) and the pentagonal *asmalyk* (literally, "hanging," Illus. 21G) decorated animals. The *khalyk* (Illus. 21H) decorated the bridal litter on the back of the processional camel, and door surrounds or *kapunuk* (literally, "for the door") proclaimed the weaving abilities and the tribal affiliation of the inhabitants of a particular yurt. These and many other genres of weaving served symbolic and practical functions in the Türkmen encampment, where weaving was not only an art form but an entire way of life.

Some collectors and scholars consider Türkmen rugs to constitute the latter-day survivors of the purest and most ancient of all rug-weaving traditions. Many of the concerns of rug scholars and collectors today—the application of structural analysis as the essential determinant of provenance, the search for accurate ethnographic information and terminology, the search for a "unified field theory" of carpet design origins in central Asia, and the emphasis on contextual information about rugs—originated in large part among aficionados of Türkmen rugs, some of whom consider themselves to be the elite of rug collectors.

21. Various types of Türkmen rugs used in the nomadic encampment (A–F by function, giving both Türkmen name and the use of the pieces)

A. Ensi, used as door of the yurt

B. Chuval, large bag hung in interior of yurt

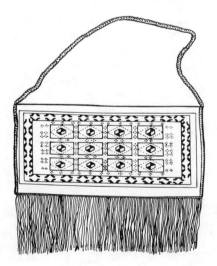

C. Mafrash, small bag hung in interior of yurt

D. Torba, medium bag hung in yurt

F. Ok-bash, used to hold stakes, spindles, or to crown tent-pole

E. Kejebe, large animal trapping for festivals

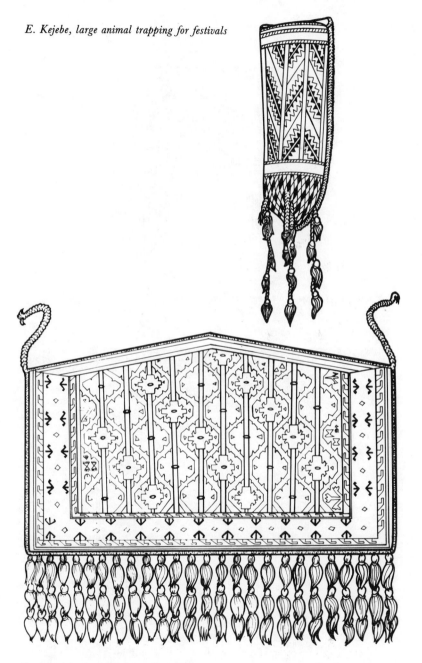

G. Asmalyk, pentagonal camel-trapping

111

H. *Khalyk, "veil" used on bridal litter on camel back*

I. (and facing page) Tentband

TÜRKMEN RUGS AND COLLECTORS

How did this situation come about? Why are Türkmen rugs—of all the major groupings the one that exhibits no securely datable examples from before the eighteenth century, the one most recently discovered by collectors, the one remotest in geographical origins, and at first glance, the one most limited in color range—the focus of such intense scrutiny and such extreme feelings? It is a temptation to explain to the novice that Türkmen rugs are like very rare and expensive burgundy wines, which they resemble in color and price. One could also add that they are a taste that, once acquired and developed, often brings the collector to the brink of both obsession and bankruptcy. Much simpler explanations probably come closer to the truth: Türkmen rugs are largely divided on the basis of structure and elements of design into six fairly well defined groups, with just enough wild cards to make life interesting. They have an enormous range of genres and functions, which are almost all well known, and their designs show provocative similarities with those of nomadic and village rugs from Iran, Transcaucasia, and Anatolia. To these explanations we might add three others: Türkmen rugs come in an abundance of the small formats favored by many collectors; there is an extremely level playing field in Türkmen scholarship; and good Türkmen rugs are—to use a quaint term—ravishingly beautiful.

THE RUGS OF THE SIX MAJOR TRIBES

Türkmen rugs were for years known as "Bukhara" rugs in the marketplace, probably because Bukhara, like Shiraz and Bergama, was a major collecting point for their embarkation on the byways of the rug market. The rug trade manufactured its own names for subgroups, such as "Royal Bukhara," applied to carpets with Tekke designs, and "Princess Bukhara" to weavings with Salor designs. We now know that Türkmen rugs—from large floor carpets ("main carpets") up to twenty feet in length, to small bag faces where the term *nine-by-twelve* refers to inches and not feet—are the product of six major tribal groups that have inhabited Türkmenia and surrounding areas during the past centuries. These are: (1) the Salor, a tribe that tradition and historical sources both indicate to be the oldest and most influential in terms of rug-weaving; (2) the Saryk, the only Türkmen tribe whose weavers used the symmetrical knot exclusively; (3) the Tekke, by the nineteenth century the largest and most powerful of the tribes, the conqueror of the Salor and Saryk; (4) the Yomud, whose wide migrating territories ranged along the eastern shore of the Caspian from Gurgan in Iran to Khiva on the Oxus delta; (5) the Chaudor, a small northern tribe whose weavings in some ways resemble those of the Yomud; and (6) the Ersari, whose range extended into Afghanistan in the south, and some of whom settled at an early date in villages along the Oxus. Branches of some of these tribes came south and west to Iran and Anatolia in the eleventh century as soldiers in the conquering armies of the great Seljuk sultans, and some eventually settled as villagers as far west as what is today the Aegean coast of Turkey, and as far south as Kerman.

A. COMMON CHARACTERISTICS

There are several basic features that distinguish Türkmen rugs. The predominant color is almost always madder red, in variations from dark walnut brown to brilliant scarlet. In common with with other nomadic weavings, wool (and sheep and goat hair), sometimes augmented with small amounts of silk or cotton, is the prevalent material for both the foundation (warp and weft) and the pile of Türkmen rugs. And a very sizable proportion of Türkmen weavings use as designs the repetition of small medallions in stacked or staggered rows, known as *gül*. In the rug literature, the word means "rose" or "flower," and rhymes with the French *nul* or the German *Mühle*. These small medallions form what were evidently symbols or blazons of individual tribal groups. In early Türkmen collecting, all one had to do was memorize six basic types of güls, and presto—one could attribute to a specific tribe any Türkmen rug with such a design.

115

B. PROBLEMS OF ATTRIBUTION

Fortunately (for the people who write books about Türkmen rugs, at least), there has been a wholesale retreat from this overly simplistic view of Türkmen weaving. Life among the Türkmen, like life everywhere else, turned out to be much more complicated. The fortunes of tribes rose and fell; sometimes one group was conquered by another, and its güls and other designs were taken over as a kind of trophy. The mystique associated with the güls of particular tribes—the Salor especially—meant that their designs were borrowed and adapted by others. Although we now believe that surviving examples can document at least 200 years of continuous weaving among the Türkmen, we still have no written history to help us deal with these beautiful works of art. Until now no documented very early examples are known to have survived. So Türkmen collecting, starting as a simple exercise, became complex, arcane, and sometimes even quasi-religious. All this was fueled by translations, usually into the mysterious language of German, of the work of obscure Soviet collectors and anthropologists written in the even more mysterious language of Russian. Most interesting of all, however, was the transliteration of words from the nonwritten Türkmen languages into Russian, then from Russian into German, and finally from German into English. The Türkmen priesthood developed its own arcane mysteries with terms like *tschowal* for *chuval,* and distinguished authorities battled over the difference between *gül* and *göl* at international conferences.

Despite all of this, the sun continued to rise in the morning and set in the evening, and Türkmen rugs continued to be beautiful just as they continued to rise in rarity and price. Amid all of the rhetorical smoke, there was some real scholarly fire as well. Today, the basic tribal groupings beginning to be established on a basis that includes both structure and design, the terminology is gradually being sorted out. From the rather limited spectrum of Türkmen rugs known by the authors of the first Türkmen books back in the 1920s, we have today entered a vast Türkmen universe, with myriads of "problem pieces" alternately attracted and repelled by the galactic gravity of the six major groups. Türkmen rugs are not only a combination of the known and unknown—they are nomadic rugs often woven with a fineness and precision that surpasses Iranian city rugs. While they apparently exerted an enormous influence on the history of weaving, one tribe at least, the Ersari, also showed a talent for expropriating rug designs from Türkmen and non-Türkmen sources alike. In short, there is something for everybody: rug paradise.

For collectors, what are the major areas of interest in these Türkmen weavings? The most important works on Türkmen rugs, encyclopedic in scope, can deal with the arcane complexities of shared designs, "borderline" pieces, the presently still little-understood hierarchy of güls, and the sometimes blurry differentiations among the rugs of the six tribes. For our purposes, it makes more sense to look at the *general* method of "typing" Türkmen rugs according to tribe, by considering a few disparate types of rugs from various tribal origins.

C. TWO BAG FACES

An old (probably late-eighteenth-century) Salor rug, formerly the front of a large horizontal bag about 3 by 5 feet, can serve as our starting point (Plate 14). It was hung on the interior wall of a yurt to hold clothing or other possessions, and was called a *chuval*—literally, "sack." A utilitarian object to be sure, it also has a very grand design of six octagonal güls with characteristic projections outward and inward from their periphery. These distinctive forms were at one time thought to constitute the major defining characteristic of Salor güls. Now we know better; Salor güls like these are found almost exclusively on Salor chuval bags only. The far more important Salor main carpets used an entirely different kind of gül. Moreover, so potent was their symbolism or magic that Salor güls of this chuval type were from the mid-nineteenth-century onward appropriated by weavers of the Saryk and Tekke tribes. Eventually, they would be produced by Beluch, Shah Sevan, and Kurdish weavers as well.

Let's return to our chuval. What then makes this a Salor piece, the prototype for later imitators? The answer lies in several things. First, the construction: The rug is robustly constructed, with around 200 kpsi, asymmetrical and open to the left, with alternate warps depressed. Second, the combination of colors: The centers of the güls are ornamented with magenta-colored silk, and the "Salor red" wool is brilliant and lustrous. Third, the proportions: In common with most older Salor pieces, the ratio of knots per inch vertically and horizontally is close to 1:1. This means that the güls are virtually as high as they are wide, in contrast to those ornamenting a later Tekke chuval, where the practice of packing down the knots and spreading the warps flat on one level has resulted in a form markedly less high than it is wide. Not firmly identified in the collecting world as authentic Salor pieces until around 1980, such rugs as this Salor chuval constitute a kind of Holy Grail for Türkmen collectors.

Let's turn to another bag face, this one in a design at first quite similar to our Salor piece; it is around the same size, and shares many elements of design with the Salor. But in fact, the knot structure is quite different (asymmetrical knots open to the right), the knots have been hammered down to make the forms much flatter, the colors are radically different, and the piece is generally thought to be a Tekke piece that incorporates the Salor design as a kind of "spoils of war" following the conquest of the Salors by the Tekkes in the 19th century.

D. THREE MAIN CARPETS

Much easier to identify for novice collectors are the orderly and for the most part predictable "main carpets." Three examples, a Tekke (Plate 45), a Salor (Plate 14), and an Ersari (Plate 15), serve to introduce us to the richness of variations on the basic Türkmen theme. The Tekke example is approximately 10½ by 6½ feet, including wide tapestry-woven bands, known as *elem,* at the ends. The field is dominated by rows of Tekke "major" güls, quartered by the thin blue lines that typically divide the entire field into a grid. The diagonal opposition of pairs of white and red quarters in the güls gives a diagonal visual flavor to the stacked rows, four wide by ten long. Between the "major" güls are the "minor" güls, which are defining elements of Tekke design. The border is composed of repetitive compartments filled with octagons, but the motifs separating the octagons show an amazing variety. While the field of the rug appears to be one of brown-red hue only, close examination shows the subtle "vibrato" of abrash in horizontal bands. The number of colors in the rug, including two reds, two blues, blue-green, yellow, brown, and white, is actually greater than that of many Turkish or Transcaucasian rugs. In addition to its structure, with asymmetrical knots open to the right, elements that define this rug as Tekke are the color, texture, grid of blue lines, variety of "separators" on the borders, and both major and minor güls.

The Salor main carpet (Plate 14), while superficially similar to the Tekke, presents an entirely different approach to the same theme. Rather than being linked by gridlike blue lines, the elements of the design "float" on the fiery-red ground of this main carpet. Also missing its *elem* ends, the Salor carpet has different proportions, being 10'9" by 8'10", and the border is much narrower and less complex than that of the Tekke carpet. The ribbed back, the asymmetrical knot open to the left, and the particularly brilliant hues, dominated by the ruby red of the field, together with the simpler and more elemental forms of the gül elements, define this carpet as the product of Salor weavers.

Finally, the Ersari main carpet (Plate 15) has a totally different character than the other two. It is over twice as long as it is wide, an indication that the weavers may have been settled folk rather than nomads; the characteristic gül forms, while used in some Ersari weaving, have here been abandoned except as small octagonal medallions in the field; the border and field designs are adapted from elements of the *herati* pattern (Illus. 22) so beloved of Iranian weavers to the south and west. The dominating madder red, the bright yellow that is found in many Ersari weavings of this group, and the coarser weave and longer, more lustrous pile, are all determinants of this rug's association with settled Ersari weavers from villages along the banks of the Oxus river. Although this rug uses the characteristic Ersari dark brown wool warp, its ultimate fall from nomadic purity is found in the use of cotton in the wefts, a technical feature also borrowed from Persian city weaving.

22. *The "herati" pattern of rosettes, plamettes, and leaves, a common pattern in Iranian carpets*

E. COPING WITH COMPLEXITY

In characterizing Türkmen weaving, the three-way comparisons we have just made illustrate the combination of easy and difficult criteria for identifying a specific tribe. In some senses, the supposed elitism of Türkmen collectors may be deserved, for more than any other group of rugs, these weavings defy definition on the printed page, either by words or by illustrations. And no group of Oriental rugs better illustrates the premises that we developed in the opening section of this book: Rugs are an art form for the sense of touch as well as sight, a knowledge of how rugs are constructed is vital for deep understanding of their artistry and origins, and in the end there is no adequate substitute for direct experience of the work of art.

OTHER WEAVING TRADITIONS

In addition to the four major traditions of Anatolia, Transcaucasia, Iran, and west central Asia discussed here, many other rug-weaving traditions, less well known by collectors, are potentially of collecting interest or have been collected by a discriminating few for some time. The older rugs of China, for example, hold considerable interest. Unlike our four major groups, they come from a non-Islamic culture, and their entire repertoire of designs partakes of a distinctively Chinese symbolic vocabulary, with unusual genres. For example, the "pillar carpet" (Plate 46) was designed to be wrapped around a vertical column; its design of a dragon, which is a Chinese symbol for the cosmos, would then appear to be coiled around the architectural element. The central Asian rugs woven in eastern Turkestan, like the culture in which they were woven, stand between the Chinese East and the Islamic West, and show a complex mixture of symbolism, colors, materials, and techniques. Both pile rugs and flat-woven examples are woven in Tunisia, Algeria, and especially in Morocco. Here, the distinctive Berber rugs of the Middle and High Atlas Mountains are created in a wide variety of techniques, while the city rugs of Fez and Rabat often show design affinities with the Iranian and the Anatolian weaving traditions, respectively.

Traditional rug-weaving in Spain ceased some centuries ago, as did the great Mamluk weaving tradition of Egypt, but in northern Iraq and Syria there are little-studied local traditions among the Kurdish population. According to historical sources, a great deal of traditional weaving was produced in the Ottoman-dominated Balkans, vestiges of which survive today in Romania, Macedonia, Poland, and Bulgaria. These and many other rug-weaving traditions are in large part waiting to be discovered, and the few specialist collectors in each area must be caught in an interesting dilemma, between wanting to share their knowledge and the beauty of their carpets, and trying to keep the collecting competition to a minimum!

CONTEMPORARY CARPETS AND THE COLLECTOR

Rug collectors have traditionally shied away from modern Oriental carpets made during the collectors' lifetime, although a few individuals collect what are sometimes called "superfine" rugs, such as the extremely finely woven products of Hereke, Nayyin, and Isfahan that are based on classical designs. The carpets woven in India in the 1950s and later after designs by Miró, Picasso, or Matisse are certainly Oriental in their geographical origin, but they tend to fall outside the scope of this book. Still there are other categories of contemporary rugs that today are beginning to be noticed by collectors, and while they are not exactly "must buy" items in the view of traditionalist collectors, they meet two tests of traditional collecting interest: (1) They are designed and made in traditional rug-weaving areas, and (2) they form a part, on one level or another, of the great historical tradition of rug-weaving that links them to the distant past.

A. RETURN TO TRADITION

On one level, and a very fundamental one, are the new rugs using traditionally dyed wool coming out of Turkey. From the pioneering DOBAG cooperative come rugs in a wide variety of impeccably traditional designs that have roots in the region where the rugs are woven, even if they have been researched in museums and university libraries in Istanbul. On a technical level, such rugs are woven in the same designs and use the same techniques, types of looms, traditional dyestuffs, and kinds of wool as the rare and high-priced antique examples from the same areas. There are differences, of course: Their colors are very strong, because they have not undergone the subtle, graceful aging that the old pieces have experienced through wear, through the corrosion of brown wool, through exposure to air and light, and through repeated cleanings. And in the attempt to uphold the standards of the old designs, the cooperatives may enforce a certain rigidity in the designs so that there is little variance from example to example. But on the other hand, the slogan once used in radio advertising by a Boston dealer—"the (new) rug of today is the antique of tomorrow"—was never truer than when applied to these new but traditionally made carpets. Moreover, they have one enormous advantage over the older rugs: They are obtainable for a tiny fraction of the price. No wonder, then, that some collectors have found such "antiques of tomorrow" of interest beyond their attributes as floor covering.

B. THE "NEW ANTIQUES"

Recognizing the demand for expensive old rugs, certain highly talented and very knowledgeable entrepreneurs in Europe, the United States, and the Middle East have gone a step further in exploiting the traditionalist renaissance in Turkey. Their success suggests that the practice may in time spread to other traditional weaving areas, especially Iran. These individuals have used the skill of Turkish weavers and the aesthetic and intellectual appeal of traditionally dyed wool, together with its prospects for graceful aging, to produce copies of certain old carpets from other, non-Anatolian traditions that command a high market price. Halfway between the "decorator" and "collector" markets, these rugs are woven in designs selected and specified by dealers in the international market, based on the demand for design types in the auction houses and dealer showrooms of Germany, England, and the United States. To satisfy collector taste, they are sometimes (but not always) subtly altered chemically to enhance the appearance of age, and the blacks may be selectively trimmed for the same effect. The result may be a copy of a large 10-by-14 Serab from northwest Iran, or a 6-by-9 Kazak from the south Caucasus, that for all except the most discriminating connoisseur has 90 percent of the visual reward of the original at 10 percent of its price. Viewed strictly as an economic proposition, such a rug looks mighty good, especially if its prospects of graceful aging mean that in fifty years it will look even more like the pricey original than it does today.

So the traditionalist revolution has created what may in the next fifty years turn out to be an entirely new collector market that in the future may create some problems of authentication and determination of age for the experts. Much the same can be said about the NEP rugs from Transcaucasia discussed earlier (see page 86). Since this is a problem the writer of this book won't have to cope with, he can view these new rugs with a combination of great intellectual interest and bemused emotional detachment.

The traditionalist revolution, centered for the moment in Turkey, has led to the creation of another kind of contemporary carpet that to this point has shown little appeal for traditional collectors, but whose future may be a different story. In various parts of the carpet-weaving world, new generations of artist-designers, often trained in urban universities or in schools devoted to the fine arts, are turning away from the internationalism and the international critical ethos of art. In a search for their own cultural roots, they are returning not to the letter, as it were, of their national artistic traditions, but rather to the spirit exemplified in earlier traditions. Some of the entrepreneurs involved in the re-creation of old artistic masterpieces have on occasion commissioned new designs that for the carpet traditionalist may at first seem somewhat jarring, but that on reflection incorporate, sometimes in dramatic and interesting ways, the flavor of the past.

C. NEW DESIGNS AND OLD TECHNIQUES

In another interesting development, artists trained in modern art schools in rug-weaving countries are experimenting with new forms that use inspiration from art of the past as the basis for radical new adaptations of designs. For example, the Turkish designer Belkis Balpınar—who started her career in textile design at the Academy of Fine Arts in Istanbul and then went on to a successful career as museum curator and director, carpet scholar, and author—has returned to designing contemporary kilims. It is not an easy task to respect the past without becoming a slave to it, or to risk sterility and stereotyping in designs; it is not an easy task to work on the cutting edge of the art of one's own time, and at the same time maintain a respect for tradition. This difficult artistic challenge is increasingly being confronted by artists in the Middle East today. In the case of the new generation of carpet designers, their success or failure will to a great extent be decided by the direction that carpet collecting takes in the next two decades, as the supply of old carpets dwindles while the fascination exerted by the medium continues to rise.

D. "ANTHROPOLOGICAL COLLECTING"

One last area of collecting of contemporary rugs is the emergence of what we might term the "anthropological collector." This is an individual who finds in the brightly colored contemporary nomadic rugs of Turkey, in the carpets from Afghanistan depicting Soviet helicopters, Kalashnikov rifles, and all of the other symbols of modern warfare that have ravaged that country, or in the variegated contemporary weavings of High Atlas Berbers the documentation of a particular way of life and a particular way of looking at things. These rugs may on occasion incorporate strident, nontraditional colors that set a traditionalist's teeth on edge; they may even show the impact of magazine advertisements, or television, or modern machines of war. Whatever beauty they may be presumed to possess may be at marked variance with accepted standards of "high" taste promulgated today by critics, professors, curators, and traditionalist collectors. But such rugs, without intellectual pretension, are exactly what they appear to be, whether that involves naïveté, artistic ineptitude, rejection of traditional values, or even simple and unadorned ugliness. And often such rugs also document the dramatic changes in traditional society wrought by the economic, social, and cultural whirlwinds of the late twentieth century. While over the long term "ethnographic" or "anthropological" collecting and art collecting have a problematic and complex relationship, it is an indisputable fact that there are today serious collectors of Afghan "war rugs" pursuing their goals in the rug market; there are also those who collect "lion rugs" from Iran patterned after British army blankets. The verdict to be rendered on this type of collecting by history will no doubt be interesting, but this writer will prudently avoid any attempt to predict the future course of the history of taste in either East or West.

CHAPTER 7

HERE AND HOW TO PURCHASE ORIENTAL RUGS AND CARPETS

INTRODUCTION

Up to this point, we have talked about "the market" in very vague and general terms. We know that many rugs were, and are, woven to be sold, and that other rugs made to be used by weavers and their families eventually found their way to the market as newer rugs were woven to replace them. For some, the market conjures up a picture of an Oriental bazaar, and indeed many experienced collectors do find their way to the traditional rug marketplaces of Istanbul and Marrakesh—although Isfahan and Kabul, for the present at least, suffer from a dearth of foreign buyers. But just as we saw that early carpets from the Middle East were common luxury items in Europe, so today the rug market is an international phenomenon, and "the market" is almost everywhere.

To be perfectly frank, the rug market has not always been popularly characterized by a reputation for honest pricing policies and straightforward representations of merchandise, a stigma it has traditionally shared with the used-car business. In the Iran-contra hearings, one U.S. government witness characterized a group of devious Iranian negotiators as "rug merchants" (prompting an angry letter to the *Washington Post* from the Oriental Rug Retailers of America). To call someone, in France, a *marchand de tapis* is not to praise his honesty and probity. Let's remember that we are looking at a market in objects that are handmade, one-of-a-kind, and made in faraway places—and except for new pieces, where the wholesale market has a standard per-square-foot rate for a given type and quality of rug, there really are no "standard" prices or price "guidelines." Rugs are surrounded by myth and traditional lore; they are artifacts of distant and misunderstood cultures, and the buyer is often at an extreme disadvantage in expertise compared to the seller. So the first piece of advice to be given is so shopworn and ancient that it is often expressed in Latin: *caveat emptor;* "let the buyer beware."

Having said this, however, it is important to add that although it is sometimes difficult to find all the great rugs one wants, at any price, it is very easy for most people with an interest in rugs to find great friendships beyond price—and many of these new friends will be in the rug business. Given that the very nature of the product means that deception (fakes and forgeries; chemically and physically altered products; misrepresented age, provenance, type, artistic attributes, and quality) is possible, it is quite unfair to characterize the entire retail carpet business on the basis of traditional stereotypes that often were based on racial or religious prejudice, or on the dishonest actions of a few. At any rate, the retail antique Oriental rug business today is in the main characterized by knowledgeable dealers who often have assimilated both traditional lore and the latest academic thinking, and who know that in order to sell fine-quality merchandise at top prices to intelligent and discriminating collectors, nothing succeeds in business like openness, accuracy of information, and factoring the element of repeat business into the pricing equation.

THE RETAIL DEALERS

Two major historical developments lie at the root of the retail rug business as we know it today in Europe and the United States. The first was the invention of the modern retail store and the large department store in the nineteenth century, made possible by a new kind of architecture and lighting, a new internationalism in buyer taste, and a dramatic rise in safety and speed of international trade accompanied by a drastic fall in its cost. The second was immigration: In the great population migrations that affected the Middle East as the Ottoman Empire collapsed and ancient ethnic rivalries erupted anew in the nineteenth century, some Middle Easterners, especially those who had commercial contacts and a knowledge of Western markets, the personal vision and expertise necessary for economic self-support, and who viewed their prospects in the countries of their birth as without much promise—immigrated to Europe and North America. There they used their commercial contacts and retail experience to enter the rug business. Many of these individuals were of Armenian descent, such as Habib Bogigian, the pioneering Boston rug dealer who sold carpets to such great New England luminaries as Henry Wadsworth Longfellow. Many of these immigrants opened small independent businesses; others took over the rug departments of the great department stores. In an age when rugs were primarily purchased in the West as floor covering, the new immigrants were a major factor in molding taste, and today many of their descendants continue as movers and shakers in the retail rug business. By the 1930s, retail dealerships in both contemporary rugs and the nineteenth-century "semi-antiques," with the Armenian-American dealers now joined by many others, were established all over the United States, but serious collecting focused on the East Coast. The older "fine art" firms, such as French and Company in New York, worked in the tradition of the great European dealer houses, such as the Munich firm of Bernheimer or the Florentine firm of Benguiat that sold great classical carpets along with European tapestries and furniture. Even dealers in old-master paintings, such as the famous Joseph Duveen, sold the occasional classical Persian carpet as the ideal decorative complement to a Poussin or a Rembrandt; after all, had not the august Viennese art historian Riegl himself stated that a Tabriz could be as great a work of art as a Tintoretto? Beteween the World Wars, the carpet trade was basically divided into two echelons of different status and with different clienteles: the "fine art" dealers and the "rug dealers." The serious interest in later carpets, at first as a collecting complement to the classical pieces, began to blossom during the 1920s, and inevitably the ranks of dealers were augmented by former collectors like Arthur Urbane Dilley, who, fascinated by the entire subculture of rugs and the rug market, became dealers themselves.

It is interesting to see the role played by the department store and the small carpet retail shop in the era between the World Wars. Here is George Hewitt Myers, destined to become the greatest collector of carpets and textiles of the twentieth century, looking in a small shop for something to put on the floor of his dormitory room at Yale, a purchase that would eventually lead to the establishment of The Textile Museum in Washington. Here is a young executive from the Naylor Pipe Company, Joseph V. McMullan, innocently walking into a Madison Avenue rug shop in New York City and striking up a conversation with fellow customers, who infected him with the highly contagious collecting virus that would one day lead to a huge gift of carpets to the Metropolitan Museum of Art. And over here is the Boston Brahmin Willoughby H. Stuart Sr., a man with a marvelous eye for color and design, buying a spectacular Milas *sejjadeh* in the rug department of Jordan Marsh that would one day belong to the Harvard University Art Museums. When the popular taste for Oriental carpets declined during and after World War II, many of the traditional dealers broadened their product line into (pardon the expression) broadloom and (excuse my language) linoleum and vinyl flooring, but they often kept their own interests in the old Oriental rugs alive as well. At the same time, those prescient collectors who had confidence in their own taste and solace in the reassuring company of each other helped to keep the flame of rug-lust alive.

An example of the influential Armenian-American dealer who influenced many collectors was Richard Markarian of Cincinnati, whose fortune, made from selling industrially produced floor covering, allowed him to build up many great Oriental carpet collections in the Middle West, including his own. By the late fifties and early sixties, rug dealers like Markarian were supplying American collectors with nineteenth-century rugs of superb quality, and some of the stars among their clients in the second generation of American collectors were even profiled in a famous article in *Fortune*, the premier magazine of American business and finance. Rug collecting was also mentioned in a front-page article in the *Wall Street Journal*.

The dominance of dealers in the collecting arena began to change in the late sixties as a third generation of collectors, many of whom had traveled in the Middle East or who had lived there as students, discovered both rugs and the rug literature. With limited budgets, great energy, and a voracious appetite for good rugs, these newcomers, many of whom were graduate students, newly minted professionals, or young businesspeople, were converted to collecting by exhibitions sponsored by the second generation. They quickly found that many of the traditional rug dealers and most of the traditional rug literature provided information that was often neither consistent nor reliable. The refusal unquestioningly to accept traditional information, the hallmark of this third generation of collectors, put them in a curious position with regard to the traditional retailers. Many of the new collectors obtained not only their first rugs, but much of their basic information, almost literally at the feet of their mentors— the traditional retail dealers. But the new collectors rapidly began to compete with these same dealers at *their* sources of old pieces: the country auctions, yard and garage sales, and out-of-the-way antique shops that in the sixties and early seventies provided a rich source of rugs but an extremely meager font of rug knowledge.

Today, retail dealers remain the most important source of carpets for many collectors, especially those outside of New England and the Middle Atlantic states. The few old-time immigrant dealers still alive continue to be a great source of traditional rug lore, and continue to inspire young collectors with their enthusiasm and hands-on knowledge. Today, it is a common sight to find in a rug shop a bookcase full of the latest publications on carpets, including exhibition catalogs, scholarly books, the major journals such as *Hali,* and above all the beautifully illustrated catalogues from the major European and American auction houses. Today's retail dealer who sells rugs of interest to collectors is more likely than not quite well informed by reading, by attendance at symposia and exhibitions, and by travel to the Middle East. The information explosion and the ease and economy of overseas travel have not only opened up the rug market to new dealers from all walks of life—from ex-bankers and ex-doctors to ex-curators and ex-poets, almost all of them incidentally ex-collectors—but have dramatically increased the level of knowledge in the marketplace. The result is a two-edged sword, for while greater knowledge on the part of dealers may assure a steadier supply of quality rugs for collectors, outstanding bargains have become rarer. Today, the collector encountering a rare old kilim in an out-of-the-way antique shop is likely to encounter along with it a price established by last week's auction sale in Germany.

In the last two decades, major carpet dealers with an international clientele have begun to imitate the practices of the major auction houses by publishing and selling, sometimes annually and sometimes more frequently, beautifully produced and lavishly illustrated catalogues of their rugs. Since this involves committing one's reputation and expertise in writing, such catalogues have the practical effect of increasing a prospective buyer's confidence, as well as providing a good source of general information for collectors. In addition, some dealers have commissioned scholarly articles to accompany their catalogue volumes. Unlike auction catalogues, however, the items illustrated in these dealer publications have frequently already been sold, and estimates of prices are often not included. These printed volumes are good advertising and provide a permanent record of the dealer's stock—and on occasion even prove to be lucrative in book sales. One drawback of these books is that, as most were published privately and without channels of distribution apart from dealer mailing lists, advertisements in specialist magazines, and specialist bookstores, those books with valuable scholarly information almost never enter academic libraries. Thus, they rarely reach an audience beyond the highly specialized collector and dealer. On the other hand, subscribing to these often very pricey series is a good way to see some of the best—and costliest—of what is on the rug market.

Of course, the average collector cannot hop an airplane to Munich or London (or to New York, for that matter) on a regular basis. After all, money spent on airfares and hotels is money not spent on the rugs themselves. A good way to see firsthand the quality and type of carpets sold by particular dealers is to scrutinize the lists of exhibitors at the major national and international antiques fairs, where some of the most prestigious dealers often have booths displaying their best wares (and their publications as well.) International art and antiques fairs in Maastricht, Chicago, and New York, whose dates and exhibitors are publicized in advertisements in the major magazines of the art market, often feature outstanding carpet dealers from all over the world. However, the prices will be equally outstanding. At any rate, at such fairs one can sometimes see the stock of up to a dozen major international dealers on one air ticket. Trade fairs, such as the annual exhibitions put on by the Oriental Rug Retailers of America, are a very good place to learn about rugs, especially about contemporary production. The periodic International Conferences on Oriental Carpets, usually held every three years, are always accompanied by dealer exhibitions (as well as by hordes of collectors with rugs to sell or trade).

THE AUCTION HOUSES

Two types of auction firms regularly hold sales of Oriental rugs: art auction firms and specialist auction firms. The major international art auction houses, such as the firms of Sotheby's and Christie's (whose London and New York branches hold rug auctions several times a year) sell everything from old masters to jewelry and musical instruments. Their carpet sales are handled by specialist departments, and are accompanied by lavishly illustrated catalogues with many color plates. The carpets are available for viewing on a specified schedule in advance of the sale, and with a few exceptions one is allowed carefully to touch and examine them. Conditions of sale are rigorously specified in the catalogues, and the authenticity and condition are attested in very specific ways. Certain standard practices, such as the inclusion of a "reserve" price under which the rug will not be sold, are explained at the beginning of the catalogue, and estimates of the range in which the final price will fall are printed in the catalogue for each item. Moreover, on request the house will send a price list after the sale that specifies which rugs were "bought in," or which failed to make the reserve price and were unsold. In major catalogue sales, the auction house in effect "puts its mouth where its money is" by making very specific representations in advance of the sale about the works to be sold, adding substantially to the confidence of prospective buyers. Carpets deemed to have lesser artistic or economic stature may be included in second-tier sales, where the more affordable prices and informality are designed to make novice collectors feel more comfortable. While their lower prices do indeed make them attractive to novice collectors, the paradox of such sales is that the works of art themselves may on occasion be more problematic, and thus require greater, rather than less, expertise on the part of prospective buyers.

1. The Regional Auction House Another type of art auction house where rugs are sold is what we might term the *regional house,* whose sources of works of art and whose clientele are primarily regional rather than national or international. Such firms may also have specialist departments, and on occasion the quality of their sales puts them on a level with the international firms. They often schedule rug sales to coincide with the major New York sales, for the convenience of European buyers and others who must travel a great distance. At their best, the regional house catalogues, departmental expertise, and works for sale can be on a level with those of the international firms. Like the big houses, the regional houses regularly advertise in the rug magazines and in major magazines covering the art market.

2. The "System" Auction   A third type of art auction sale, closely related to the first but under greater government control, is the "system" sale, a type that originated in France. In Paris such sales are held in the famous Hôtel Drouot, and in Vienna in the Dorotheum. The basic system consists of the auction firms themselves, known in France as *commissaires-priseurs,* who for the purposes of writing the sales catalogue enlist the services of an *expert,* an individual who has been certified by examination as an authority in the field. The presale exhibitions and the sales themselves are held in the government-owned auction house. While sales of rugs at such institutions can be extremely interesting, the most important European carpet auctions, for a variety of reasons, tend to take place either in the international houses in London or in the specialist auction houses throughout Europe.

3. Specialist Auction Houses   The specialist auction firms are relative newcomers to the field, starting in London and New York in the 1970s with the now-defunct firms of Lefèvre and Edelmann, auction houses that sold nothing but Oriental rugs and textiles. These firms also advertise in the major rug journals, and their sales, accompanied by handsome catalogues, are said to be highly successful.

The catalogues of rugs published by major retail dealers (mostly in Germany) and by the major auction houses in Europe and North America have undergone very interesting transformations in the last two-and-a-half decades that quite accurately reflect changes both in the market and in the field of collecting. As the level of knowledge about carpets has risen, so has the quality of information provided by sales catalogues, some even including state-of-the-art structural analyses of important pieces and expensive color illustrations in numbers about which most museum curators and scholars can only dream. This does not mean that such catalogues are immune from the occasional howler, such as the invention by the rug department of a London auction house of the "Gapylyk" tribe *(gapylyk*—or *kapılık*—means "for the doorway," a term discussed in our section on Türkmen rugs) or the term *Kum Kapour* that persistently, against all logic, still appears as a title for rugs woven in the Kum Kapı ("Sand Gate") quarter of Istanbul. But as a general principle, the catalogues of the major retail dealers and auction houses, while expensive, are of great usefulness to serious collectors; subscriptions to the latter can be had by writing directly to the auction houses, while copies of the former can be found in specialist bookstores.

ESTATE AUCTIONS

Estate auctions are often excellent places to buy Oriental carpets—especially in parts of the United States such as New England, where Oriental rugs were once a standard part of the traditional furnishings of elegant homes. Every rug collector cherishes the hope of arriving at an estate auction in the rural hinterland to discover some rare and costly treasure whose true value is unknown to the auctioneer and the audience of local people. There was a time, remembered with immense nostalgia by the author, when such events actually did occur. Today, however, when one pulls up to the tiny rural farmhouse full of exquisite rug treasures in East Ayuh, New Hampshire, the first two languages one is likely to hear as one disembarks from the family car are Persian and Brooklynese, spoken in accents not-so-sweet by a swarm of pickers. The term *picker* is not one favored by these individuals themselves, who prefer *dealer*.

In practice, a picker is someone who serves as a sort of commercial intermediary between the established antique rug dealer and some of the sources of the dealer's stock, moving through the vast ocean of rural and urban antique shops, country auctions, garage sales, and backyard clotheslines in search of rugs. These individuals usually do not own stores, and while many do have a few collector clients, they commonly count on quick turnover of limited working capital by selling to retail dealers, to each other, or to the collector that they have just outbid at the East Ayuh farmhouse. No serious collector will *ever* turn down an invitation to look in the trunk of a picker's car.

Pickers have one aim in common: to buy as many of the rugs as possible without paying too much. In practice, this leads inevitably (and often illegally) to the *ad hoc* buyer's cartel known as "the ring" or "the coalition." To avoid bidding against each other, members of the cartel will appoint one individual to bid for all of them, up to a particular level determined in advance. After the auction is over, they will pay what they owe to the auctioneer (who usually insists on cash) and then hold their own private auction, the "knockout." Here, according to a mathematical formula, some members of the ring will end up with rugs, and others will end up with cash. The behavior of members of the ring often adds interest to an otherwise dull country auction— especially if a major misunderstanding takes place, affording the scholarly onlooker an opportunity to brush up on the latest street argot of Qazvin or Queens.

For the collector, the chief drawbacks of the estate auction are: (1) not having any real idea of the number and quality of the offerings until you arrive; (2) having to travel some distance over unfamiliar ground to get there; (3) buying rugs "as is," and running the risk either of spending too much for one with an irremediable defect, or missing the buy of the century because it was filthy and hard to examine under the hay baler; and (4) being at a geographical disadvantage with regard to the local inhabitants, and at a psychological disadvantage with regard to the vastly more experienced pickers.

A further risk of the estate auction is the practice, not unknown, of "loading" a sale. While the sale may be advertised as "Property belonging to the late Augustus Terwilliger of East Ayuh, New Hampshire," some of the rugs may actually belong to an out-of-town rug dealer who has persuaded the auctioneer, on the basis of many years of close friendship, to include in the sale all of the rotted, painted, shortened, patched, and otherwise fiddled rugs that he cannot sell in his shop without misrepresenting them. The practice of loading sales clearly creates disadvantages for the prospective buyer. Knowing your auctioneer—and remembering the classic dictum "You trust your mother, but you cut the cards"—are good precautions. The best advice for estate auctions is to preserve your emotional distance; you should attend such an auction with your hopes well tempered by pessimism, and avoid rash behavior unless you can very well afford it.

"FLYING CARPET" AUCTIONS

One last type of auction is to be considered here. One usually finds out about such auctions through a newspaper advertisement usually resembling the following:

BY ORDER OF THE DISTRICT COURT OF EAST DUBUQUE
AND THE UNITED STATES BUREAU OF CUSTOMS
DOCKET #3456-789012

UNRESERVED AUCTION SALE

EIGHT BALES OF RUGS SEIZED FOR NONPAYMENT OF DE-
CIDUOUS DEBITS AND FISCAL TURBULENCE IN THE PRE-
EXISTENT MONETARY FIDUCIARIES OF THE CONFLATED
EXTRANUMERARIES OF SHANGRI-LA LTD. INTERNATIONAL

Including examples of: Kashan, Silk Kashan, Kerman, Royal Im-
perial Kerman, Kazvin, Kilim, Monjour, Gapykyk, Soumak, Silk
Koum Kapour, Waterbug-Border, Royal Bokhara, Princess Bokhara,
Yarmouth Bokhara, Hamadan, Lilahan, Bilmem, and Anlamam,
Certified and Licensed by Notarized Affidavit as Being Genuine
Hand-Woven Oriental Rugs Woven by Certified and Licensed Hands.

FOR SALE TO THE HIGHEST BIDDER WITHOUT RESERVE
AT PUBLIC AUCTION AT THE VACATION MOTEL,
555 Shad Row, Nevertell, N.J.

TERMS: CASH OR CERTIFIED CHECK

The best advice about attending such auctions with serious intent to buy rugs is: *Don't!* Those with sufficient time to spend on broadening their anthropological knowledge of the wonderful world of selling may find attendance interesting, but leave your cash and certified checks at home unless you are very sure of yourself. There are two potential problem areas with such sales. First, the auctioneer is generally not from your area, so obtaining your legal rights as a consumer, should the dyes in your bargain antique Bejizostan stain your oak floors a bright red, or the pile in your overpriced Royal Imperial Kashan disappear into the bowels of your Electrolux, may be a difficult task. And second, it is not unheard of for some auctions of this type to involve a "shill," someone who works for the auctioneer and poses as a potential buyer, "bidding up" items that attract the interest of legitimate buyers.

MISCELLANEOUS VENDORS

Rugs of interest to collectors can be found almost anywhere. While antique shops, used-furniture stores, and emporiums specializing in imports are the usual suspects in this regard, the dyed-in-the-wool collector *never* stops looking. The vast treasure-house of collector lore is full of anecdotal evidence for the mysterious existence of a Divine Carpet Providence, my own favorite being the magnificent little Shah Sevan sumak-brocaded bag face found in a florist's shop. Still miraculously intact, it served as a sort of doily under a large potted palm. The "locked trunk" stories are too numerous to relate, but the alleged contents of these mysterious containers, always supposedly purchased for under $15, range from great medallion Ushaks from sixteenth-century Anatolia, to all of the missing borders of the Ardebil Carpet now in the Los Angeles County Museum.

The experienced collector knows that a good rug may turn up anywhere, but as with the collection of any kind of art, it is extremely important to understand the difference between shopping for rugs themselves and shopping for information about rugs. You can buy rugs anywhere, but accurate information about the rug you buy is a much scarcer commodity, and the usual criteria for relying on information—the education, experience, reputation, and reliability of the source—must always be kept in mind.

GOING TO THE SOURCE

More and more, collectors of Oriental rugs are reluctant to collect at a distance from the source of their treasures. They are traveling, either in groups sponsored by museums and collecting organizations, or individually, to the countries of the Middle East where their treasured collections originated. Since in recent years travel to Iran and Afghanistan has become somewhat impractical, and travel to the states of Transcaucasia carries with it a considerable physical risk, the range of options for this type of travel is somewhat narrowed at present. Nevertheless, those who want to see rug-weaving or the present-day heirs of the great rug-weavers of yore firsthand can obtain the experience in Pakistan and northern India, in western China, in Morocco, in some of the new central Asian republics, and above all in modern-day Turkey.

As mentioned, the advent of the fax machine, express mail, and inexpensive international direct dialing means that for some items prices are the same in Van, Turkey, and Vancouver, British Columbia, but if you want to see and learn about a lot of Berber rugs, you still have to go to Morocco. And if your interest is in older Caucasian weaving, the rug markets of Turkey are currently the place to be. Foreign travel to the source is also useful to the collector for two other reasons—it gives one a fundamental, gut-level idea of how values on the market are determined, and the great carpet markets and museums of Istanbul and (perhaps again some day) Teheran are among the best places in the world to learn about rugs.

CHAPTER 8

OW TO UNDERSTAND PRICE, VALUE, AND THE MARKETPLACE

INTRODUCTION

One of the most essential aspects of rug collecting, of course, is that of economics: determining the fair market price of a particular carpet at a particular time. Price guides for the art collector, both general and specific, appear from time to time in print. Nevertheless, such works, as useful as they may occasionally be in a broad, general sense, cannot possibly take into account all of the objective factors like condition, dyestuffs, or wool quality—let alone the equally important subjective ones like beauty, originality, or relationship to historical context—that have such important bearing on the price of any work of art. So we have a problem: How does the collector, especially the novice, get some idea of price structure in the market without having the services of an expert appraiser at her/his elbow twenty-four hours a day?

In our technological society, with all of its faith in "experts," perhaps the most important thing to realize is that there is no infallible determination of monetary value in art. Nor is there even often much consensus among the experts, *nor has there ever been, nor will there ever be.* Even the rug specialists at the major auction houses, where knowledge of price structure is an important requirement for one's job, cannot accurately predict the hammer price of every rug all of the time. Simply compare the preauction estimates published in any auction catalogue with the postauction price list, and look at the discrepancies. And as for those books that purport to tell you how to make money in the rug market, let's ask the obvious question: Why is the author sharing these secrets with you for the price of a book?

The second concept with which new collectors sometimes have problems is the entire notion of "value" itself. This is a book about collecting art, and not about speculating on the art market. Therefore, it is possible to offer for the collector some basic advice and some sound principles with regard to allocation of finite monetary resources in an often bewildering market for rugs and carpets.

FIRST STEPS IN COLLECTING

The first thing for a new collector to acquire is knowledge about the ebb and flow of fashions and fads, and of supply and demand in the marketplace, for which there are many useful resources. The best place to begin is in the retail marketplace itself; getting into the habit of *regular visits* to the local dealers of your choice, and discussing with them the collectible rugs that they have in stock, including price, is the most reliable way of getting a handle on the rugs themselves. At a retail dealer's you can examine rugs closely, you can compare several side by side, and you can usually ask questions and learn about the object of your interest. Some dealers, or course, are reluctant to discuss price and desirability with someone they perceive not to be a serious or sophisticated buyer, and there is a long tradition of secrecy about prices in the retail business. Some dealers don't price the merchandise with a tag at all, but instead give the rug a number; they then match with entries in a notebook listing the price they paid for the rug in question—there are usually no "sticker prices" here. Unfortunately, some dealers are unwilling to discuss either rugs or prices in the context of educating a client. When a dealer responds to your query about the price of any rug by asking how much you are willing to pay, the only intelligent response is to turn your back and walk out of the store. But most dealers will discuss price with individuals they deem to be serious about purchasing rugs; the flexibility of prices, a not uncommon feature of the art market, may leave some room for negotiation.

The first way to establish communication, of course, is to come into a rug store with as much knowledge as possible—to have a good general idea of what you are looking for, and how to go about looking for it in a stack of folded or rolled rugs. This at first involves knowing what kind of rug you want the dealer to unfold or unroll for you, and later evolves into your being able to recognize yourself, from the back in a pile or roll, the rug or rugs you want to see.

The second aid to communication, which stems from the first, is to convince the dealer that you are a serious person with serious interests, who in exchange for information is seriously interested in buying rugs, and not someone who is trying to get a free education at the dealer's expense. Once some common ground for communication is established, you can proceed with enjoyment and ease. In the case of a new collector, the best tactic is simply to declare both your interest and the fact that you are a beginner who is willing and eager to learn. Also, you have to remember that many dealers in old rugs have vast amounts of both knowledge and enthusiasm, and know that imparting both of these is good for business. In addition to knowledge, three things help in collecting: money, energetic hunting, and good interpersonal skills. The most successful collectors rely primarily on the latter two.

Plate 17. The Virgin and Child Enthroned, Gentile Bellini, Venice, ca. 1480 C.E. Oil on Panel, 48″ × 32½″. Reproduced courtesy of the Trustees, The National Gallery, London (NG3911).

Plate 18. Mosaic Felt Rug, Türkmen, Afghanistan, 20th Century C.E. Detail. Toronto, Royal Ontario Museum, 976.244.

Plate 19. Pazyryk Rug, 4th Century B.C.E. 74″ × 79″.
St. Petersburg, Hermitage.

Plate 20. Carpet with Geometric Arabesque, Anatolia, 14th Century C.E. Detail.
Istanbul, Türk ve Islam Eserleri Müzesi, Inv. 685.

Plate 21. Carpet with Chinese Textile Design, Anatolia, 14th Century C.E. Detail.
Istanbul, Türk ve Islam Eserleri Müzesi, Inv. 688.

Plate 22. Carpet with "Small-Pattern Holbein" Design, Anatolia, 15th Century
C.E. Detail. Istanbul, Türk ve Islam Eserleri Müzesi, Inv. 303.

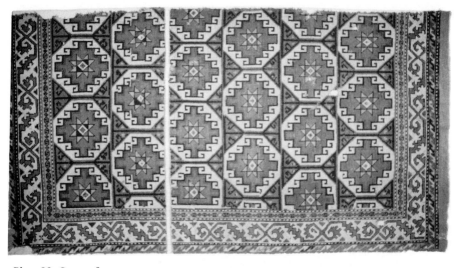

Plate 23. Carpet fragment with "Memling" Design, Anatolia, 15–16th Century C.E. 67″ × 37″. Budapest, Iparmüvészeti Múzeum.

Plate 24. Carpet with "Large-Pattern Holbein" Design, Anatolia, 16th Century C.E. 115″ × 67″. Istanbul, Türk ve Islam Eserleri Müzesi, Inv 468.

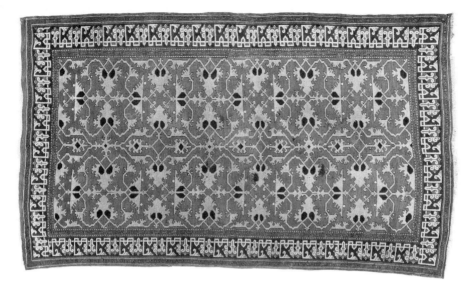

Plate 25. Carpet with "Lotto" Design, Anatolia, 15th Century C.E. Detail.
Philadelphia Museum of Art, The Joseph Lees Williams Memorial Collection.

Plate 26. Fragment of Carpet with Ottoman "Saz" Design,
16th Century C.E. 38″ × 37″. The Textile Museum,
Washington, D.C., R34.33.2.

Plate 27. The Ardebil Carpet, Iran, dated Hegira, 942 (1537 C.E.). 34'6" × 17'6".
By courtesy of the Board of Trustees of the Victoria & Albert Museum, London.

Plate 28. Mamluk Carpet, Egypt, ca. 1500 C.E. 82" × 71". The Textile
Museum, Washington, D.C., R16.2.2.

Plate 29. Carpet with Double-ended Triple-arch Design, Anatolia, 18–19th Century C.E. 80″ × 66″. New York, The Metropolitan Museum of Art (1974.149.20). Bequest of Joseph V. McMullan, 1973.

Plate 30. Mucur (Mujur) Prayer Rug, Anatolia, 19th Century. 5′6″ × 4′. Cincinnati, The Markarian Foundation, No. 26.

Plate 31. Yastik (Cushion) Cover with 4-Leaf Design, Anatolia, 19th Century
C.E. 34″ × 21″. Private Collection.

Plate 32. Carpet with Dragon Design, Transcaucasia, 17th Century C.E. Detail.
The Textile Museum, Washington, D.C., R36.1.2.

Plate 33. Kazak Carpet with "Large-Pattern Holbein" Design, South
Transcaucasia, late 19th Century C.E. 249 × 198 cm. Courtesy of the Harvard
University Museums, No. 1980.62. Gift of Dr. Alfred Farah.

Plate 34. Karabagh Carpet with "Sunburst" or "Eagle" Design, South
Transcaucasia, late 19th Century C.E. 6'10" × 4'8". Courtesy of Sotheby's.

Plate 35. Shirvan Carpet with "Pole Medallion" Design, East Transcaucasia, late 19th Century C.E. 97″ × 50″. Courtesy of Sotheby's.

Plate 36. Daghestan Prayer Rug, North Transcaucasia, late 19th Century C.E. 63″ × 53″.

Plate 37. Mughan Rug with "Memling" Pattern, Southeast Transcaucasia, 19th Century C.E. 94″ × 42″. Courtesy of Sotheby's. 6407–139.

Plate 38. Tabriz Carpet with medallion design, Northwest Iran, late 19th Century C.E. Detail. Courtesy of Sotheby's.

Plate 39. Sehna Carpet with "Herati" Design, West Iran, late 19th Century C.E. Detail. Courtesy of George Walter Vincent Smith Museum.

Plate 40. Bijar Carpet with "Rumi" arabesque design, West Iran, late 19th Century C.E. Detail. Courtesy of Sotheby's.

Plate 41. Kashan Carpet with medallion design, Central Iran, late 19th Century C.E. 79″ × 55″. Courtesy of Sotheby's.

Plate 42. Kerman Carpet with design depicting great historical and mythological personalities. Approx. 10′ × 14′. South Iran, late 19th Century C.E. Courtesy Koko Boodakian & Sons, Winchester, MA.

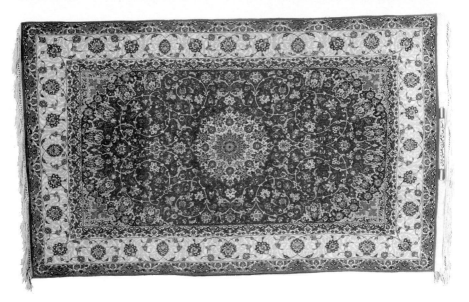

Plate 43. Isfahan Carpet with medallion design, Serafian Atelier, Iran, mid-20th Century C.E. 93″ × 57″. Courtesy of Sotheby's.

Plate 44. Bakhtiyari Double Flour Bag, Iran, early 20th Century, one side. Approx. 3′ × 4′. Private Collection.

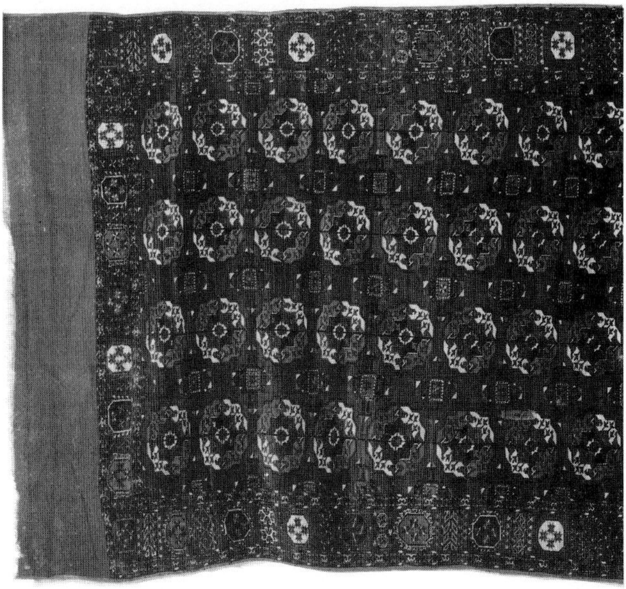

Plate 45. Tekke Türkmen Main Carpet, West Central Asia, 19th Century C.E. Detail. 97″ × 75″ plus flat-woven "elem" at ends. Courtesy of Sotheby's.

Plate 46. Pillar Carpet with Dragon Design, West China, 19th Century C.E. 109″ × 59″. Courtesy of Sotheby's.

Plate 47. Modern Turkish Kilim, designed by Belkis Balpinar, ca. 1990. Approx. 8′ × 5′. Private Collection.

Plate 48. Tekke Türkmen Chuval Tent-Bag, West Central Asia, early 20th Century. 29″ × 47″. Owned by Walter Denny.

GETTING A GRIP
ON FADS AND PRICES

No individual dealer's stock of collectible rugs can possibly give you a complete idea about the overall structure of the present market, although dealers themselves are always very much aware of what is currently hot among collectors. To obtain this information independently, there are a number of very reliable and useful sources.

DEALER CATALOGUES

The first place to look, especially if you can't regularly attend preauction exhibitions and the sales themselves, is in the auction catalogues, together with the published price lists put out by the auction houses. Subscriptions to auction catalogues can be obtained by writing the auction houses; some public and research libraries also have both current and past catalogues.

PUBLICATIONS

Beyond this, there are several periodical publications specializing in carpets that include surveys of recent market prices and discuss market trends and tastes. Some, like *Rug News*, are primarily intended for dealers in the decorative rug market, who sell exclusively or primarily to interior decorators. Others, like *Hali* (published six times a year in London) and *Oriental Rug Review* (published six times a year in New Hampshire), regularly review rug auctions and discuss not only the prices, but the relationship between the price and the specific rug involved. Occasionally, these periodicals even identify the buyer and discuss his/her tastes and preferences. When the pioneering *Hali* first appeared almost twenty years ago, it represented a huge step forward in informing collectors. Today, both magazines—the sophisticated, far-ranging and internationally oriented *Hali* and the down-to-earth, often scrappy and irreverent *ORR*—are valuable sources of price and market information as well as knowledge of carpet history and artistry for any serious collector.

The rug market is very strongly influenced by publications, especially when they focus on relatively new or unknown material. The book ads and book reviews in *Hali* and *ORR*, or the books promoted and stocked by specialist bookstores, are often a very good indication not only of what is of interest to collectors today, but what is likely to be the next area of collector interest. Another very useful indication of fashion is the choice of rugs that are published in color by advertisers in the rug magazines. It is a clear indication in many cases of what a given dealer believes will attract large numbers of collector-buyers. One significant exception here: Advertisements in magazines also serve to establish a sociological pecking order in the dealer subculture, and sometimes an advertisement is designed as much to influence other dealers as it is prospective collector-customers. Featuring a $100,000 rug or a sixteenth-century classical rug in an ad serves a purpose intimately related to a dealer's status and prestige; after all, both can contribute to profitable collector business, even if the specific rug featured in an ad is beyond the means of all but a very few.

MAKING THE CHOICE

Now let's consider the price of the specific rug that you have just spotted in a dealer showroom (Plate 47), a rug that not only satisfies your interest in *general type* (you happen to have a particular passion for Turkish yastık cushions), but also your interest in a *specific type* (for whatever reasons, you find most of the pieces with four stylized leaves to be very attractive, and you have wanted one for yourself for a long time). Let's say that the price tag on the rug in the dealer's shop is $600—which for a rug about 32 by 18 inches seems to you to be a hefty chunk of cash—but you have the money in your savings account, and for three nights you have dreamed about the rug.

Before beginning the whole process, you need to figure out

how much *time* you have; the major advantage that the experienced collector has over the novice is that the former can make decisions more decisively and quickly. To even things up, ask for some time. Sometimes a dealer will hold a rug for a few days—usually enough time for you to do your homework. Sometimes a dealer will let you take the rug home on approval for a few days, knowing full well that letting the rug get completely under your skin in your own home is an excellent sales tactic. Let's imagine that dealer A, the seller, lets you have the rug to look at for seventy-two hours. What do you do?

Maybe we should start by looking at what *not* to do. It is *not* wise to take dealer A's rug to dealer B and ask him about the proposed price; not only are you asking for what in essence is a free appraisal, but word gets around in the market, which is not likely to please the seller of the rug. You can, of course, *pay* another dealer or a professional appraiser for a cost estimate, but this takes time, costs money, and involves potential conflict of interest (dealer B, the appraiser, may want to influence you to use your $600 to buy a rug from him/her). In the end, all this effort doesn't help you to learn. And it doesn't deal with the most important aspect of the rug's value—its appeal to *you*. Were you considering paying over $200,000 for a seventeenth-century Persian court carpet, it would be quite in order to pay (hefty) fees to a couple of experts for their opinions. As a novice, however, you are collecting on a different level, and for a different set of purposes, including the pleasure you get out of learning and doing things for yourself.

Now, in the three days available, it is possible for you to take some time to look at other Turkish yastıks of the same general age, size, and condition at local dealers, and to compare prices. The great advantage of using this method to determine a price level is that you not only get a retail price quote, but can examine the rugs themselves—as opposed to pictures, which never tell you the full story. The disadvantages, of course, are the expenditure of time (but remember, it is time spent in *learning*) and the fact that unless you live near a big city with many dealers, at any given time there are unlikely to be a lot of closely comparable rugs for sale in your area. Let's suppose that you see in the shops of dealers B and C three Turkish yastıks that, like the object of your desire, have good colors, show reasonably good condition, and are priced around $600. You also see one yastık that is almost exactly like yours, but it is quite worn and missing about two inches from the top and the bottom, and is priced at around $100.

Let's further suppose that with the help of a friendly fellow collector, your local library, or an obliging dealer, you can look through the auction catalogues of the past few years for price estimates of Turkish yastıks in general. If you're lucky, you might see an estimate for "four-leaf " yastıks in particular; maybe you'll even be able to look at the price list from a particular sale to determine the exact price (remember to factor in sales taxes, the seller's premium, and the buyer's premium). With really good luck, you might find a mention of a comparable piece, with photo, in the auction reviews in *ORR* or *Hali*. Let's suppose that in the past year the magazines and auction catalogues recorded the sales of nine old yastıks, with sales prices of $200 (for one piece), $400 (for another one), $800 (for four, including one that in the photograph looks very much like "yours"), $1,000 (for two pieces), with the one remaining piece going much higher, for over $6,000. Such price variations for rugs of a similar size are certainly quite normal, because the variables of condition, color, and artistry are in the collector market the really important ones.

What have you learned about the price of the rug you want to buy from your survey of the local dealer stock and your perusal of the catalogues and magazines? You have found that the price quoted you by dealer A is in the low-to-middle range for roughly comparable pieces. What might be some of the reasons it is at first glance quite reasonable? First, there is the cost at which the rug was bought; perhaps your dealer bought it quite cheaply and wants to move it fairly quickly. Second, there may be factors of condition that you have overlooked—and sure enough, when you examine it again, you see that the selvedges are replacements for the original. Also, there is a small renapped spot about two inches square that was so well done you missed it at the first lookover. Third, the type may be quite common. Indeed, a friend who collects tells you that yastıks of the four-leaf kind are frequently encountered in the marketplace. These bits of information being digested, the price begins to look, in the context of the market, quite reasonable.

What else have you learned from this particular exercise? First, you have learned that condition makes a *big* difference. Second, you have learned something about availability and rarity of particular types and particular designs. Third, you have learned that extraordinary examples of particular types may sell at *far* above the median price, for reasons that are seldom readily apparent. This probably has as much to do with the psychology of two individuals present at a particular auction as anything else. Fourth, you have learned that with a little time the novice collector has a lot of potential help to fall back on—and in the end, this will enable you to build both your knowledge and your confidence.

By now, you are getting close to the point of buying the rug. There remains, however, another group of questions that you had better confront. Unlike the *what, when,* and *how* questions you have already answered, this group is a much more psychologically complex one: the *what if* questions. What if I buy this yastík today, temporarily emptying my savings account, and tomorrow I find something I like much more? What if I ask the dealer if he will take $500? Do I risk blowing the entire deal? What if I find an identical piece next week for $300? What if I have missed some terrible defect in the rug, or I have made some gross error of aesthetic judgment, or have somehow failed to realize that this rug is not an old Turkish yastık, but a modern Dutch reproduction?

There is not a collector in the world who has not experienced the existential agony of the "what if" crisis—usually just as he or she has pulled out the checkbook. Learning to trust one's judgment takes time, and it helps to have a record of success as well. Just remember that if you *like* the piece, if you have made prudent and reasonable inquiries to make sure that it is what you want it to be, and if you have reasonable confidence in the dealer, then waiting for a better rug to come along is pointless. There is always a better example somewhere, but you are making your decision in *your* market and at *your* moment. Yes, you may find an almost identical example next week for $100 less—it often happens, but so what? You also may never see another example at such a low price for the rest of your life. That often happens, too. Learning to overcome a bad case of the "what ifs" is part of maturing as a collector.

Far more important a matter to consider as you approach a decision to buy is a reevaluation of the rug of your choice *in the light of what you have just learned*. When you saw the rug seventy-two hours ago, you fell in love with it. Since that time, you have seen four more examples "in the wool" and over a half-dozen more as illustrations in books. You have perhaps read something about the design and its origins in old Ottoman silk cushion covers, and in looking for information on this particular type of rug, you have also probably looked at least obliquely at a lot more rugs of many different types. Is the magic still there? If it is, take the plunge! And remember that it is quite normal for a new collector to buy things that, years later, may be sold or traded for other things. Your taste will change. But for today, it is important to remember the old adage: "A Bijar in the hand is worth two that you haven't seen yet."

A CHECKLIST OF PRACTICAL QUESTIONS FOR THE BUYER

A. THE INTEGRITY OF THE SELLER

Do I trust this person or this firm? Has he/she/it been established in business in this place for some time? How open was he/she about pricing? How open and forthcoming about the rug and its type? Did he/she point out any problems with the rug as well as its attractive aspects? Do I know other collectors who have dealt with this firm satisfactorily, and have recommended it as a good source for rugs? In addition to that afforded to me by the laws of my state, is there any additional buyer protection, like a buy-back or exchange guarantee? Many dealers, in order to encourage customer confidence, are quite creative about such matters.

Another matter that may be of some significance is the professional standing of the dealer or firm. National associations of dealers, for example, seek to maintain high standards of integrity in the marketplace—and a firm's membership in such an organization, and adherence to its policies and standards, may be a substantial aid to establishing confidence on the customer's part.

B. THE CARPET AS AN AESTHETIC OBJECT

Is the carpet really attractive to me? Are the colors satisfying, the design without annoying glitches, the "handle" and the wool to my liking? Is it a pleasing and interesting representative of its type as to its genre, geographic origin, and age? If there is an artistic pedigree, does the carpet form a lively part of the story of evolution and stylization? What will the carpet look like in my living room, or hanging next to my other carpets?

C. THE CARPET AS AN ECONOMIC OBJECT

Is the price within a reasonable range for such carpets? Can I buy this carpet and keep some financial flexibility for the next nice example to come along? At this stage in my development as a collector, is owning this carpet a reasonable and attractive means of apportioning my limited money resources?

D. THE CARPET AS A PHYSICAL OBJECT

Is it really what it appears to be?

1. Integrity of the Fabric Turning it over, do I see evidence indicative of reduction or augmentation in size; has it been shortened or narrowed, or have two carpets been grafted together in some way? Have patches from other rugs been inserted into the fabric? Are the warp and weft strong, without weakening or disintegration caused by dry rot? The old test of folding a carpet and then compressing it, listening for the telltale "popping" of weak, dry-rotted warps and wefts, is sometimes not easy to do discreetly in a dealer's showroom, but if you suspect dry rot, you should ask the seller to guarantee that there is none.

Is the carpet missing something from the ends, and if so, is this a factor in its value or appearance? Are the edges worn, or has the selvedge been replaced—and if so, is this significant for the rug's structural stability, appearance, or value?

2. Colors and Pile   Are the colors fresh and true, without unattractive fading, strident shockers, ambiguous hues, or other indications of poor-quality dyes? Is the abrash (the natural color variation of traditional carpets) subtle and enhancing of the rug's beauty, or is it harsh and abrupt? Is there evidence that the colors have been chemically altered, or that the blacks have been trimmed down rather than having corroded naturally? Is the pile in good condition, and, if there are patches of wear, are they visually significant? If the pile is worn, is the wear patchy (which is normal) or very even overall (which may suggest that the rug has been artificially aged by grinding down the pile with pumice stone)? Is there any evidence of "painting," the direct application of felt-tip markers to the warp or weft? Has the rug been seriously re-piled, as evidenced by patches of pile with a different color, texture, or length from that of the surrounding pile? If so, has it been done well or poorly, and, given the age and type, is this significant? Remember that old rugs almost *always* show wear, repairs, or both. Finding an old rug in absolutely perfect condition, while not unheard of, is both rare and a reason for extra caution about its age.

3. Structure   Is the carpet's weaving structure appropriate to its design, age, and type? Ordinarily, in buying most kinds of carpets, it isn't vital to do a complete structural analysis, or even to analyze the knot count and type. But there are very important exceptions: For example, if the carpet is represented as a Salor Türkmen, it had better have an asymmetrical knot open to the left and a "ribbed" back, and if it is represented as a Gördes, it should usually show a random pattern of diagonal lines, sometimes called "lazy lines," on the back. Such lines result from the wefts being passed only partway across the carpet by the weaver, then doubled back. The once-popular Gördes carpets were copied in many places and, as we have seen, Türkmen designs were often borrowed by one tribe from another.

4. Materials   Is the carpet made from the appropriate materials? Are the warps cotton or wool? (You can best familiarize yourself with the difference by examining the fringes of new rugs that use both.) Are they appropriate to the purported type and origins of the carpet in question? If not, do they suggest that the carpet is a copy or that it has been restored on the ends? If the carpet has been represented as having silk pile, is it really silk (not "floss silk," "imitation silk," rayon, mercerized cotton, or other "silky" euphemisms that are not really silk)? There is no easy way to answer these questions in a book—you have to learn by looking together with someone, usually a reputable dealer, a teacher, or a fellow collector, whom you can trust. Is the pile wool appropriate to the carpet (coarse, lustrous, and shiny if a Kazak; fine, long-fibered, and soft if a Kashan)? Sometimes carpets were woven of wool removed from the hides of slaughtered sheep by a depilatory, rather than shorn from living sheep with shears. Such "dead wool" or "skin wool" is often dry to the touch and lifeless and dull to the eye. Finally, remember that almost no collector knows all of the answers to all of the pertinent questions at the time of buying, nor does he/she have either the knowledge or the time to answer all of these in every case. Sometimes a collector encountering something exciting but unknown is forced to fall back on "instinct," when a quick decision is essential. Time and caution are always vying with each other when you have an important collecting decision to make, and it is not always possible to satisfy both. The balance you strike between the two will be totally individual to you, depending on two things: your personality and your pocketbook.

COPING WITH AND LEARNING FROM YOUR MISTAKES

If you spend all your time worrying about making a mistake, you'll never enjoy or succeed at collecting; sooner or later, errors are made by every collector. The purpose of increasing your knowledge is to avoid making serious mistakes whenever possible, but mistakes are often educational as well as sometimes being a bit expensive. To this point, we have concentrated on telling you how to avoid mistakes. What about coping with them?

The first rug bought by the author of this book (Plate 48), looked to him like a rare Salor Türkmen; it was actually a much more common Tekke. It appeared to have good colors; in fact, there was an aniline red that ran profusely when the rug was washed. The rug appeared to be intact; instead, it had been narrowed by several inches. It appeared to be an old example; as it turned out, it wasn't at all. The type of dye used wasn't perfected in a European chemical factory until around 1900. In one single purchase, I had made most of the common mistakes that a novice collector makes. The first was misidentifying the type of carpet by relying only on design, which I had compared with a small black-and-white illustration in a book. The second was not carefully examining the structural integrity of the carpet to see that it had been skillfully reduced in size by a vertical cut on the right side, probably to avoid the re-napping of a hole. The third mistake was not carefully examining the color of the carpet and the dyestuffs. There were telltale pink stains on the stripped white warps at both ends. The fourth error was not having had a series of similar objects for comparison, which would have easily demonstrated to me that the carpet was a very late example in the sequence of design evolution. And finally, I did not have a piece of knowledge that emerged only in the 1980s: Real Salors are distinguished by a very specific structure of warp level and knots, regardless of their design. Making all of these mistakes at once was a piece of luck; it involved enough cash to be acutely embarrassing without being financially disastrous, and it meant that I was "sensitized" to some fundamental issues at the very beginning of my collecting career. Also lucky for me was the fact that I was then twenty-four, and my mistakes increased my interest in collecting rather than diminished it.

Having made a mistake, how do you cope? You may choose, as I did, to hold on to the carpet in question as a memento of your mortal fallibility, a kind of symbolic hair shirt for your collecting sins. Most of the time, however, we want to remove from our sight (and from our living premises) the evidence of our rash or stupid behavior. Sometimes coping with our mistakes involves honestly reselling or trading the unwanted rug, and swallowing the financial loss. If the rug in question has been misrepresented by a dealer or auctioneer (remember our earlier discussion of "conditions of sale," which are printed at the beginning or end of an auction catalogue), it should be returned within a stipulated time for a refund. In most states, the definition of misrepresentation is not confined merely to making false statements about the rug, such as misrepresenting a Hamadan as a Kashan. It also applies to errors of omission, such as neglecting to tell you that the rug with serious dry rot that you purchased today had been returned to the dealer the day before by another customer for the very same reason.

More arcane questions of attribution, involving knot structure and the like, are less susceptible to such redress, since the authorities may disagree or the distinctions on which the attribution is based may appear in literature unknown to the dealer (or to you) at the time of purchase. Being egregiously overcharged for a rug is another question. New rugs—those in production today—usually have a standard wholesale price per square foot determined by the particular type and quality. In the case of antique pieces, there is considerable latitude as to what constitutes an appropriate price, but if you have some evidence, such as a closely comparable piece selling for considerably less in the same geographic area at the same time, you may attempt to return the rug for a refund. No dealer wants a reputation as one who grossly overcharges susceptible customers, and a forceful presentation of your case in this regard may produce satisfactory results. On the other hand, be very wary of deciding that you have been snookered by dealer A simply because dealer B says he bought a similar rug for one-tenth the price. Unless the purchase was made in the same general market at the same time, and the two pieces are *really* similar, that may not be true. And what kind of a retail markup did dealer B put on the piece, anyway? There is *always* a difference between buying price and selling price, and there is usually a difference between the price of an old rug in a rural tag sale and the general retail price of comparable objects on the world market, depending on how well informed the tag-sale proprietor is. Every dealer dreams of finding a quarter-million-dollar Star Kazak for $20 in a tag sale, but that doesn't mean he has to sell it to you for forty bucks. And besides, as a collector you have the same dream of making the same killing, don't you?

In collecting, making mistakes is simply a component of learning, and while serious mistakes should be avoided or redressed, the sort of judgment errors that we all make in collecting should be examined, analyzed, and then factored into future decisions. With experience, most collectors learn increasingly to trust their own judgment, and with increasing faith in one's own judgment comes increasing pleasure from collecting.

DEMEANOR AND BEHAVIOR
IN THE MARKETPLACE

Going to a major rug auction at one of the big auction houses can be an exciting experience. Around you in the crowd are many of the major dealers and collectors, reporters from the major rug and antique magazines, authors and authorities of one kind or another, and an almost tangible atmosphere of excitement and anticipation. Also around you are countless psychological "subtexts" and personal dramas—the actings-out of individual relationships of trust and fear, love and hate, ego and insecurity, that characterize all human interaction. Such forces seem to appear in especially raw and unrefined form when the collecting lust is so strong that you can almost smell or taste it.

The experienced collector quickly learns, however, that the masking of one's raw emotions is for most individuals an essential part of collecting success. Remember that while demonstration of your *general* enthusiasm for carpets may help you to form a good relationship with a dealer, the urge to show *particular* enthusiasm for a carpet you haven't bought yet should be tempered with restraint. It's simply unwise to inform a dealer that you can't live without a particular carpet he has for sale. Nor is it very helpful for you to look at the rug with dilated pupils, heavy breathing, small beads of sweat on your forehead, and other tokens of unrequited longing. Try to keep cool, both literally and figuratively.

Once you have mastered an air of moderate boredom and polite indifference, remember that if it comes to bargaining for a rug, you should not embark on the process unless you are seriously intent upon buying that particular rug at a particular price. Avoid making an offer that is clearly ridiculous; you should have a clear and informed idea of how much the rug is worth and how much you want to pay before you start. Otherwise, you risk jeopardizing the development of mutual trust and respect that is a necessary prelude to a satisfactory relationship between dealer and client. No reputable rug dealer has the time or the patience to put up with ignorance, disrespect, rudeness, or dishonesty on the part of a customer, any more than you have the time and patience to endure this treatment from a dealer.

And finally, in addition to appropriateness of behavior, the experienced collector learns that in the marketplace, *listening* is almost always preferable to *talking*. It is fun to sit around and listen to collectors and dealers bragging about their sales triumphs and extolling their superior intelligence and discrimination, but don't make the mistake of joining in. In the marketplace, you are interested in acquiring not only rugs, but experience and knowledge, and none of the three should be given away without some firm guarantees of reciprocity. The *real* experts know that they always have something new to learn, and in the marketplace new things to learn almost always outnumber old rugs for sale.

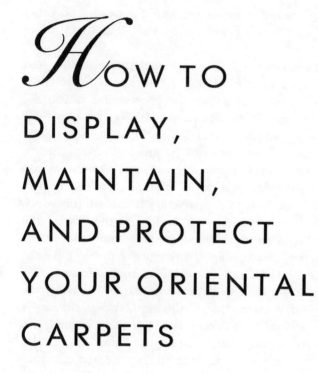

CHAPTER 9

How to Display, Maintain, and Protect Your Oriental Carpets

Introduction

From the trade journals of the carpet-cleaning industry to the technical literature of the scientific field of textile conservation, there are many publications that deal with the cleaning, conservation, and museum display of carpets, but it is not our intention to attempt to duplicate that information here. We do want to answer a few basic questions that the carpet collector, whether novice or established "rug bug," may have about cleaning, conserving, storing, and displaying rugs—as all of these things make demands on a collector's resources.

Displaying Your Collection

FLOORS

Traditionally, carpets were and are sold to be used as floor covering in European and North American interiors. Many collectors continue to display their rugs on floors, although they usually take measures to minimize wear and dirt, such as keeping rugs away from heavily trafficked areas or adopting the custom, common in traditional rug-weaving areas, of exchanging street shoes for slippers at the entrance to the house. Rugs kept on the floor should be cushioned by rug pads. The old felt rug pads common twenty years ago, while their thickness made rugs susceptible to wear at the edges, were otherwise excellent for floor use. These have given way to thinner pads made of vulcanized rubber (not recommended for valuable rugs, because of their tendency to decompose and because of their sulfur content) and pads made of various new polymers and other materials. Ideally a rug pad should do two things: (1) It should cushion the rug from being ground between two hard surfaces: the soles of shoes and the floor; and (2) it should keep the rug from slipping. It should accomplish these goals without being too thick (causing high edges and a danger of tripping) or prone to disintegration or to adhering to the floor or the rug.

While their often large size and unsuitability for horizontal hanging make it a temptation to display kilims on the floor, the great fragility of such rugs makes this practice extremely unwise. The same is true of all fragile carpets, whether flat-woven brocaded rugs, or seriously worn or "thin" rugs with weak foundation structures (including old Sehna pieces with their single wefts and silk warps). Silk rugs should *never* be displayed on floors.

Finally, the collector should consider the other activities that take place on top of rugs that are displayed on floors. The old Victorian institution of the "dining-room rug," generally a handsome medallion carpet whose design was hidden under the dining-room table—and which was abused by chairs being skidded back and forth and by constant baptisms of greasy food and staining drink—comes from the same dark and sadistic neighborhood as the debtor's prison and the insane asylum. The same thing might be said for the practice of putting flowerpots and planters directly on rugs. This is an open invitation to dry rot resulting from overwatering and spills on the rug. Moreover, some plant-borne insects actually like to eat rugs, too. Decisions about pet-free, plant-free, child-free, and food-and-drink-free, or shoe-free zones are difficult to make, but it makes little if any sense to spend $10,000 on a carpet as a work of art, and then abuse one's trusteeship of the work and deprive future generations of its beauty. Bits of food and drink, while themselves potentially destructive of carpets, carry the additional hazard of making the rug a tastier treat for moth larvae, crickets, and silverfish. Rugs kept on the floor should be regularly cleaned by vacuuming on *both* sides, periodically rotated, and given a washing on a regular basis as necessary. They should also be checked periodically for evidence of insect infestation, which can be brought into the house by pets, guests, flowers, or food. It's a very dangerous world out there.

FURNITURE

The old rugs depicted in European paintings of the sixteenth and seventeenth centuries were commonly shown on tops of tables and other pieces of furniture. Small rugs in particular are easily displayed in this fashion, but they should be protected from the depredations of food and drink, and from candle wax and other similar substances that harm the carpet and taste to bugs like béarnaise sauce on a filet mignon. It is generally not a good idea to place a large protecting sheet of glass or plastic over a rug on a tabletop, as either can cause accumulation of moisture to occur. Rugs of unusual shape and with very specific uses and contexts, such as bedding bags or flour bags, can be displayed to advantage on frames or bolsters designed for the specific purpose and that show them in situations comparable to their original uses.

WALLS

Hanging rugs on the walls is today the preferred manner of displaying one's most valuable carpets. Preparing rugs for hanging used to involve sewing a fabric sleeve at the top of the rug, through which a rod was then inserted. The rod was then hung from a wall. The preferred hanging method in use today, widely accepted among museums and among collectors, is the use of strips of two-part "hook and eye" fabric tape, such as Velcro. The "eye" strip should be machine-sewn to a piece of pre-washed cotton uphol-stery tape, which in turn should be hand-sewn carefully to the back of the rug, preferably with linen or cotton carpet thread; the "hook" strip may be stapled to a beveled strip of wood, called the hanging flat, which can then be notched into its matching wall flat (Illus. 23). The well flat can be hung, screwed, toggle-bolted, or nailed to the wall.

This method of hanging allows the rug to be removed easily for rolling or cleaning, keeps the rug some distance from the wall, and can if necessary be complemented by other Velcro strips on the sides, and another at the bottom of the rug to keep the bottom corners from curling out or under. In principle, with the exception of certain prayer rugs (where the bottom of the rug and the bottom of the design are at different ends), rugs should be hung with the direction of the pile facing down, in order to minimize accu-mulation of dirt and maximize the effect of lighting.

In choosing a surface for hanging rugs, several important guidelines should be observed. First, it is unwise to hang rugs over hot-air vents or other places in the house with extreme temperatures and moving streams of air. Rugs should not be hung close to space heaters, coal or wood stoves, or the exit vents of humidifiers. Spotlights and other heat-producing lamps should be kept an appropriately safe distance from rugs. One should avoid hanging carpets where they are exposed to direct sunlight; ultraviolet filters for fluorescent lights and for windows should be considered. Small rugs and fragments can be mounted on cotton or linen canvas stretchers for display, and these can be glazed (preferably with ultraviolet-filtering Plexiglas or similar material) and framed.

The hanging of kilims and of fragmentary carpets presents a separate set of problems. Because large slit-tapestry kilims, some-times 12 feet in length or longer, must be hung vertically (since the wefts are not continuous across the rug, hanging them horizontally causes the slits to gape open and may weaken the fabric), one needs to have very high ceilings to hang such rugs. Other expedients include the unsatisfactory one of draping the kilim across a rod and hanging it in two halves, or the expensive option of mounting the kilim on a huge linen-covered stretcher that can be hung horizontally. Badly damaged carpets in all techniques, together with fragments, should always be mounted on stretchers to preserve and display them and to avoid further damage, such as the loss of knots or the unraveling of edges. Ready-made stretchers covered with unprimed painting canvas are available in art supply stores, as are all of the materials for making stretchers.

LIGHT AND HUMIDITY

Museums follow strict procedures in display of textiles, including frequent rotation and very low light levels. In general, traditionally dyed rugs in sound structural condition can be displayed for extended periods of time without undue worry, as long as they are protected from abrasion, dirt, extremes of temperature and humidity, and strong light—especially light with an ultraviolet component. Those fortunate enough to have more rugs than they have display space might profitably consider rotating their treasures; three months on and nine months off is an ideal schedule.

CLEANING YOUR COLLECTION

Like everything else, carpets get dirty. Since cleaning carpets itself can involve wear and tear, the experienced collector recognizes that prevention—keeping one's collection from getting dirty in the first place—goes hand in hand with the careful cleaning of one's collection. Careful display of carpets on floors, walls, and on furniture, as mentioned, can result in minimal accumulation of dirt over time. Control of environmental factors such as smoke and dirt in the air can further help to keep rugs clean. But eventually, whether someone spills a plate of hummus on your prize Perepedil, or your favorite Feraghan begins to look a

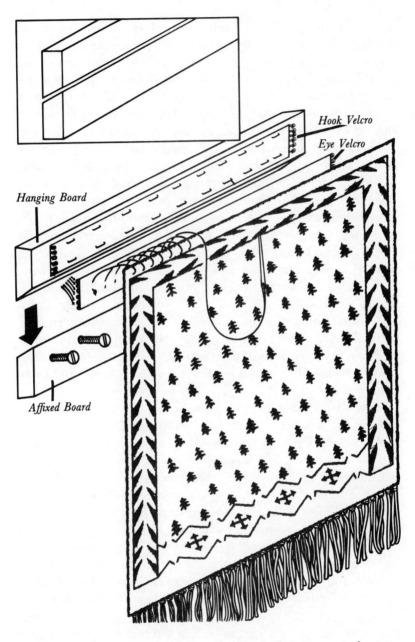

Hook Velcro

Eye Velcro

Hanging Board

Affixed Board

23. *Diagram of a common method for hanging carpets, utilizing two-part velcro tape and a two-part hanging board*

little gray and peaked, it's time to consider cleaning your rug. By "cleaning," we actually mean washing, with the modern-day equivalent of soap and water, which you can either do yourself (in the case of little pieces) or pay someone else to do (recommended for larger pieces). Commercial carpet cleaning involves huge machines that feed the carpet over giant rollers, then wash the rug with high-pressure jets of water tinctured with detergent, rinse it, wring it between huge cylinders, and then affix the rug to a hanging nail bar that is lofted into a room with circulating hot air for drying. While this process is perfectly fine for newer floor rugs in sound structural shape, your older rugs should be hand-washed horizontally with a minimum of brushing or rubbing, and then gently dried—also horizontally, or with as little stress as possible on the warps and wefts. Getting a rug wet, even after wringing, can triple its weight (remember that the fifty-pound Bijar comes out of the bathtub weighing almost 150), so gentle treatment is preferred. Many commercial cleaners now offer special hand-washing for collectibles, and some even offer state-of-the-art, museum-quality cleaning, complete with deionized water. Usually there are standard per-square-foot charges that are competitive within any given area, with a cash-and-carry discount.

If you wash small rugs at home in the tub, it is best to use a neutral-pH (neither acid nor base) detergent. One such product is the popular Orvus, a brand name for a chemical called sodium laureth sulfate that is derived from coconut oil and probably is a principal ingredient in the shampoo that you currently use. Other gentle nonperfumed soaps are acceptable, but it is absolutely vital to rinse the soap residue from the rug, and to dry the rug fairly quickly so that rot will not ensue.

The option of mothproofing rugs used to be quite popular; this once involved impregnating the rug with a toxic substance, like arsenic, that would kill the moth who tried to make a meal of the rug. Whether the same thing would happen to a puppy or a toddler at the "chewy" stage of development was not clear, but the consensus today seems to be that the best way to keep your rug from being devoured by insects is to keep it clean on both sides, rotate it regularly if it is on the floor, keep your house clean and free of bugs, and store the rug properly when it is not being used or displayed.

CONSERVATION AND
RESTORATION OF RUGS

Well, let's suppose the worst happens, and Towser chews a corner off your treasured Talish in a fit of pique. Or perhaps a gang of silverfish from hell eats the backs of the knots off your revered Raver, or your tipsy boss spills a glass of deep-red Chambertin (the '85 bottle you got for Christmas) on the Dawlatabad in the dining room. Besides confining the pet to the basement, fumigating the parlor, and quitting your job, what are you to do? In the first instance, your rug needs structural repair to its wool warps and wefts, in addition to replacement of wool pile. In the second, it needs re-napping on an otherwise undamaged cotton foundation. In the third, it needs serious and quick attention to a potentially disfiguring stain. The first two problems are jobs for a professional rug repair person: Reweaving of a hole or a chewed corner is the most expensive type of repair; re-napping is less expensive, unless it involves a very finely knotted and dense rug like a Bijar or a Kashan. Such highly skilled work is pricey, so ask for a written estimate. Avoid the offer to re-nap other parts of the pile, reselvedge the edges, and refringe the ends at the same time, unless your rug really needs it. Such offers are common during the winter, which is the slow season for rug repairers, especially in New England. Removing the stain is something you should do yourself, with the aid of one of those books on coping with household disasters. Put a bowl *under* the stain to collect the runoff, and prop the rug up so that it can dry quickly; a hair dryer can help speed things up a bit.

Over time, rugs left on the floor will need their edges and ends repaired, and areas of pile re-napped, before they wear out altogether (by now you have a rough idea about how the author of this book feels about putting beautiful old rugs on the floor). Avoid if possible the sewn-on selvedges or the machine-serging of edges that used to be in vogue. They can in a few minutes almost miraculously give a $10,000 Kashan the look of a $100 Belgian knockoff. The sewn-on, machine-made cotton fringes, some of them artfully soaked in coffee or tea to simulate age, used to be popular solutions (no pun intended) to loss of knots from the end of a rug, but they are a matter for your own taste. Costs of these repairs are usually charged on a per-linear-foot basis; avoid open-ended, hourly commitments, or at least ask for a written estimate.

STORING AND SAFEGUARDING
YOUR COLLECTION

Small rugs can be stored flat, preferably wrapped in acid-free paper in acid-free textile storage boxes. These are not outrageously expensive, and information on how to buy them is available through conservators, museum conservation departments (which are happy to oblige *contributing members* of the institution), and archival and conservation supply firms and catalogues. Larger rugs should always be stored rolled, and *never* folded. Acid-free cardboard tubes used with acid-free tissue paper are best for roll storage. Rugs should always be clean before you put them in storage. The storage place should be cool, dry, and free of insects, and rugs should be checked periodically for insect damage. Never introduce an unclean rug into a storage area, for the pests it carries will rapidly colonize the clean rugs already there. Use of mothballs is not recommended these days; they aren't very effective, smell terrible, and aren't good for your health. Aromatic wood such as cedar helps, but never store a rug in direct contact with wood whose surface has not been sealed and treated by an inert varnish like urethane, for oxidation and acid in the wood can over time "burn" the rug. Protecting your valuables from fire is a complex and expensive task far beyond the scope of this book, but giving up smoking is a good start because it reduces the danger of fire. Besides, cigarette smoke is almost as bad for your rugs as it is for your lungs.

After considering all of the everyday dangers to rugs that lurk within your happy home, it is almost with a sense of relief that we turn to the hazards of theft. Theft of Oriental rugs is not an abstract phenomenon—it is a highly specialized, highly profitable, rapidly expanding sector of the crime business, and has become so pervasive that some states and cities have established specialized bureaus within their detective forces to deal with the problem. Theft occurs everywhere. You may come home from work to find your front door bashed in and your Kermans gone; by the time you dial 911, the culprits are probably taking off from the airport on their way to Europe. You may send rugs out to be cleaned or restored, and get different and less expensive ones back. It has been known to happen, so know your rug service person and, more important, know your rugs. Many individuals take these potentially valuable possessions so much for granted ("It was under the dining-room table for thirty years, for heaven's sake . . .") that when items are stolen, the owners are unable to identify them, describe them, or give an estimate of their value. No wonder that rug theft is such a popular vocation; it is almost impossible in most cases to prove that the rug in the thief's possession ever belonged to its real owner.

While the chance of robbery can be reduced, if not averted altogether, by the usual preventive devices (locks, alarms, guard dogs, crocodile-filled moats, and mantraps), the word to the wise these days is to avoid conspicuous consumption. This means not bragging about your valuable collection to strangers. You should also exercise discretion in your choice of the individuals that clean, repair, and insure your collection, since they all know what you've got and how much it is worth. You also want to avoid feature articles on your collection in the local newspaper, and to keep unwanted salespersons from the interior of your house.

None of this, however, offers an ironclad guarantee that you may not get robbed. Should this happen, there are a few relatively simple steps you can take that will greatly increase your chances of getting your rugs back.

1. First, have your rugs *appraised* by a trusted, competent appraiser. The American Association of Appraisers, your local

museum, or your insurance agent can help you in this regard.

2. Second, *insure* your rugs with an itemized "fine art rider" on your household insurance—or, if you like the cachet, with Lloyds of London. Yes, it's a pain in the neck to prepare the list, which will require accurate dimensions, name of rug, and other information, but it's worth it for your peace of mind or should the unthinkable actually happen.

3. Third, and almost as important as the other two steps, *photograph* your rugs. With the highly automated cameras in vogue today, this is a cinch. There is no longer any excuse for not doing it yourself. Photograph the small ones by holding the rug up vertically while a trustworthy friend takes the shots. Use color negative film, preferably 100 ASA for fine grain. To get better lighting, avoid using the flash; photograph the rugs outdoors, but *in the shade,* using a skylight filter if your camera takes one. Take pictures of the entire rug, and then take details of distinctive parts, such as any inscriptions or dates, identifying repairs, unusual motifs, and corner adjustments in the design. For the big carpets on the floor, after taking a few general photos from different angles, take several detail pictures of each—including the corners and any place that the design may undergo an abrupt transition peculiar to your rug. For floor rugs, it's better to use high-speed film and natural daylight than it is to use a flash. Photograph any areas with unusual wear or repairs; these may be quite important in identifying the rug. At the same time that you photograph your rugs, measure them carefully. Order two sets of 4-by-6 color prints—on Fujicolor SFA3 paper, if you can get it—one for your picture album and one for the safe-deposit box. (The negatives and a duplicate copy of your inventory will also repose in your safe-deposit box.) If questions arise about the rug that came back from the cleaners or if the Karagashli in the entrance hall disappears with the traveling salesman (serves you right for keeping it in the entrance hall!), you will have a record of what you lost.

Making an inventory with photographs of your rugs is not only good for security purposes, but a very good way to learn more about your own collection. This is especially true if you accompany it with a written catalogue that describes each rug and gives some basic technical data on materials and structure. Some day, as part of your "doctoral degree" in collecting, you may be ready to write the definitive scholarly catalogue of your own rugs, complete with full technical analysis. Until then, the insurance inventory is a good learning experience.

CHAPTER 10

*H*OW TO INCREASE YOUR KNOWLEDGE

INTRODUCTION

For the collector, learning about Oriental rugs begins and ends with collecting itself. Looking at large numbers of rugs on the market, discussing quality and price with dealers, comparing rugs with each other, and living with the rugs one has acquired form the core of one's knowledge about carpets. But taken alone, learning in the market has some drawbacks. For one thing, it is much easier to accomplish in a large metropolitan area with many dealers, but relatively difficult in other locations. For another, the information obtained from the market is often skewed away from the historical and contextual aspects of rugs. For yet another, the market creates its own fictions, as we have seen in the case of the apocryphal "Bilmem," "Kum Kapour" and "Gapylyk" rugs, which are often not susceptible to easy rebuttal or correction in the context of the market. For this reason, almost all successful collectors use other sources of information. In addition to reading the enormously useful and informative rug magazines and auction catalogues, and the catalogues and monographs written or commissioned by dealers, successful collectors usually read other kinds of books, including those written by academics, curators, and other scholars not directly involved with the selling of rugs.

They also learn from exhibitions of carpets of many kinds: some are mounted by museums, others by private galleries, and others by collecting organizations in association with meetings and symposia. The collections in the storage areas of museums are sometimes available for study as well, either through group visits organized by collecting organizations or through private visits connected with research projects. A few museums sponsor short courses or seminars on carpets that use the collections as a basis for instruction. These are often a most valuable opportunity for a collector not only to see fine examples of carpets not often available for public viewing, but to get serious scholarly information on carpets and their history.

Collecting organizations themselves provide the serious collector with the opportunity to meet with other collectors, to share information and experience, and to hear speakers on a variety of subjects of interest. And a very few colleges and universities in the United States offer formal courses on the history of carpets in their curricula on the history of art. It is perhaps ironic, however, that in general, colleges and universities are usually the last place that a collector can turn for serious pursuit of knowledge. Even those institutions that offer courses on Islamic art usually disregard what is the most socially and geographically pervasive, economically significant, and distinctive form of artistic expression in Islamic civilization.

LEARNING FROM
THE RUG LITERATURE:
A BEGINNING

In the last two decades, there has been a great outpouring of published material on rugs in all of their aspects. In addition to magazines and dealer publications specifically aimed toward rug collectors, these include books on the rugs of particular broad or specific geographic areas; books on rugs woven in particular techniques, produced by particular tribes and tribal groups, or created for particular uses; and exhibition catalogues that may focus on one or more similar themes. In addition, there are what we term "scholarly" articles on rugs. These are usually short writings, normally focused on highly specific subjects, that appear in highly documented format with extensive footnotes or endnotes common to scholarly works in the humanities. Such articles are often published in journals sponsored by museums and universities.

To survey only the most important works in the rug literature would require hundreds of pages. In this book we have given a short descriptive list of some of the basic publications of interest to the novice collector, including recent publications still in print as of the writing of this book (see chapter 12). Many of the older standard works of interest to collectors are out of print, but can be found in public libraries or libraries of museums and colleges. Other old books can still be purchased; many are sold by used-book dealers, and the majority of these titles can be found, with some careful looking, in the catalogues or on the shelves of specialist booksellers.

In common with most art books that have large numbers of color plates, many of the best rug publications are somewhat expensive, and the experienced collector learns which books are essential for a collector's personal bookshelf and which are better used by consulting them in the library. The money so saved, of course, can be spent on rugs themselves. In assessing the value of books, the book reviews published by *Hali* or *ORR* are often valuable, as are the occasional scholarly reviews published in journals dealing with Islamic art or art of the Middle East.

In allocating scarce resources for books, there are a number of things every experienced collector considers:

1. Does the book cover material in which I am directly interested, or that pertains to the collecting tradition in which I am directly interested? There are hundreds of rug books out there, and it makes little sense to allocate your resources for books dealing primarily with fields of collecting very far from your own—unless, of course, you have made the (expensive) decision to collect rug books as well as rugs themselves.

2. Does the book present new and up-to-date material, or is it largely a rehash of other books that I already own? In other words, has the author broken new ground in this book, or is the book largely a recompilation of accepted lore and a recycling of information available in other books? There is a lot of "vanity" rug publishing, sometimes by dealers seeking to enhance their reputations, and sometimes by collectors seeking to enhance the value of their collections. These can be very useful, but the value may lie chiefly in the illustrations and not in the text.

3. Are the illustrations useful for me and my collecting interests? Are the color plates of good quality and are the captions and descriptions accurate? Are the rugs illustrated superb examples (which I can use as a standard for my own collecting) or rather, are they humdrum, ordinary examples that teach me little about quality?

4. Is the book solid or speculative? Is the author's writing based on carpets and their history, or on speculations about the origins of designs and their meanings that slant everything in the book? Is the book documented with a wide range of solid data, or based largely on what the author believes to be visual similarities between works of art produced by widely separated cultures in widely different media? Does the book provide me with information about the author's research methods and source materials?

5. Is the author him/herself aware of the recent literature, not only in English but in other languages as well? Does the book include important recent publications in its bibliography, and is the author using up-to-date terminology and building on the work of other reputable authors?

6. Is the price of the book consonant with the value of its information, both in its illustrations and in its text? Or would the money spent on the book be better allocated toward the purchase of a rug?

LEARNING FROM
EXHIBITIONS AND
MUSEUM COLLECTIONS

Exhibitions of carpets, whether they are special loan exhibitions on specific topics that are often shown at several museums as part of a touring show, or exhibitions from a museum's permanent collection that are shown in its own galleries on a rotating basis, are a very good way to learn about rugs. This is especially true of the early and rare examples that seldom show up in auctions or dealer showrooms. Loan exhibitions and touring exhibitions are often accompanied by handsome catalogues; among these are some of the most important rug publications of recent years. Special exhibitions are often accompanied by educational programs, such as symposia or lectures by noted authorities, films and video productions dealing with carpets and their context or history, and practical workshops primarily intended for collectors.

Of course, there is a great deal to be learned from the collections of museums themselves. We have listed in chapter 11 some of the major museum collections in North America and Europe. Most museums show only a small portion of their holdings at one time; carpets are, of course, often quite large, and even a large museum gallery may have space for a limited number of examples. The old practice of permanent exhibtion of carpets has been largely discontinued. In order to minimize long-term exposure to air and light, most museums now rotate their carpets on exhibition, or exhibit items from their collection on a periodic basis. Furthermore, new museum standards for exhibition mean that preparation of carpets for exhibition is costly and time-consuming, and some museums simply lack the budgetary or specialist resources to conserve their collections, let alone prepare the bulk of their collection for public showing.

Art museums are chartered (and are exempt from certain taxes) as institutions devoted to the public good, for the purpose of education and the advancement of scholarship. Consequently, the rugs in museum storage facilities are usually available for study by qualified specialists, but are often difficult for the ordinary collector to see. They require a good deal of time and physical labor to unroll, and restrictions on their handling require that a curator closely supervise the individual or individuals examining them. Under the circumstances, a museum curator might quite naturally prefer to arrange a visit to the storage areas by a group of interested collectors, rather than for one person. This depends, of course, on the amount of viewing space available. Here is where the collector organizations have been quite successful in arranging for visits to museum collections in storage. Some individual collectors and collecting organizations have "adopted" the carpet collection in their local museum, encouraging and supporting both loan exhibitions and exhibitions from the permanent collection. Some even contribute funds for the cataloguing, mounting, and conservation of carpets, and serve as volunteers to help in these tasks. In return, a museum such as The Textile Museum in Washington, D.C., sponsors regular programs for collectors, including the famous weekend "rug mornings" where collectors can examine rugs from the museum's vast holdings and compare them to similar rugs brought in on Saturday mornings by other collectors. Such symbiotic relationships serve both the collector and the institution, and they have an impressive record of accomplishment in the advancement of knowledge and collector enthusiasm and interest over the last twenty years.

And finally, some museums even sponsor guided tours led by

museum curators to the rug-weaving areas of the world, or tours that concentrate on visits to major museum and private collections in the United States and abroad. These provide interested collectors with rare opportunities to see both collections and the creation of carpets themselves, and to share the knowledge, contacts, and opportunities for access of the tour leader in a hands-on experience.

OPPORTUNITIES
FOR FORMAL LEARNING

The art of the Oriental carpet is one of the most important manifestations of material culture in Islamic society, in terms of the long and complex history of the art form itself, in terms of the importance of the form for the overall development of Islamic art, and in terms of the social and economic importance of carpet weaving in Islamic societies. For this reason, it is quite astonishing that most academic specialists in Islamic art, while extremely well versed in such arcane media as inlaid metalwork or arts of the book, know or care very little about what for centuries has been the best-known, most-appreciated, and, in Islamic society, among the most culturally significant forms of art. This curious fact is mirrored in the course offerings of college and university programs in Islamic art. Only a tiny handful of institutions offering courses in Islamic art itself (and there are few enough of those) have ever offered academic courses on the history of carpets, and only one or two include carpet history as a regular part of their curricula. For the collector, therefore, opportunities for formal learning are few indeed. Short courses offered by museums help to fill the gap; so do special courses offered through college programs in continuing education. In each case, however, it is important for the prospective student to ascertain the academic qualifications of the individual responsible for the course. For the present, however, the opportunities for pursuing formal study of carpet history in American institutions of higher learning, despite the active public interest, are almost nonexistent.

COLLECTING ORGANIZATIONS AND EDUCATION

The Hajji Baba Club in New York City, founded almost sixty years ago, was the first American rug collector organization. In the 1960s, many other groups came into being as the collecting of carpets burgeoned, and they have played an important role in both collecting and scholarship since that time. Collecting organizations sponsor important exhibitions, usually consisting of rugs drawn from the collections of members. They support publication of museum catalogues and other scholarly efforts. They sponsor regular programs of lectures, films, workshops, and visits to museum and private collections. They often provide their members with periodic newsletters giving up-to-date information about new and noteworthy publications, and some even make new books available to their members at substantial discounts by purchasing them in large quantities.

Collecting organizations are of course a good way for collectors to learn from each other, and meetings of most organizations set aside time for members to "show and tell" about their latest acquisitions, getting opinions from other members or from visiting experts. The most important information about prices and dealer reputations in the market, availability of different kinds of rugs, and the pitfalls and perils of collecting is obtained not from publications but directly from the individuals who have most recently encountered these aspects of collecting. By providing a forum for learning and exchange of collector information, the rug organizations provide a service that is for almost all serious collectors an absolute must. Membership in most rug organizations is available by expressing interest and paying dues, and it is not geographically restricted. The rug society in southern California mails its frequent newsletters to members all over the country, as do some of the East Coast organizations. Among the most active groups today are the New York Rug Society, the San Francisco Bay Area Rug Society, the Chicago Rug Society, the Washington Textile Group, the Princeton Rug Society, the Quebec Carpet and Textile Society, the Pittsburgh Rug Society, the Textile Museum Associates of Southern California, New York Hajji Baba, and the New Boston Rug Society.

CONFERENCES AND MEETINGS

In the 1970s, The Textile Museum in Washington, D.C., began holding in the fall an annual conference of rug societies. Under the sponsorship of the museum, members of rug clubs from all over the United States congregate in the District of Columbia for a conference, generally dealing with a specific topic and usually associated with a current exhibition at The Textile Museum. These annual conferences, limited in number of participants for reasons of access to rugs and the small size of the museum itself, have been for many years one of the major rug events of the year.

For almost two decades, the International Conference on Oriental Carpets, an organization formed by representatives from many countries, has sponsored conferences dealing with many different aspects of carpet history. These conferences, held every two to four years at a different site, are the blockbuster events of the rug collecting world. They are usually coordinated with major exhibitions by museums, dealers, and collecting organizations, and their programs often include dozens of speakers, sometimes running in concurrent sessions. Conferences held in London, Vienna, Budapest, Hamburg, Berlin, Washington, Munich, and San Francisco have included large numbers of participants, and have afforded them unique opportunities to see large numbers of outstanding rugs and to assimilate vast quantities of information. The scholarly papers from some ICOC meetings have been published as books, and the conference program booklets themselves often constitute a useful learning resource. The whirlwind profusion of museum and exhibition openings, receptions, banquets, films, workshops and demonstrations, and the rich mix of the market and the scholarly world continue to make the ICOC meetings a major clearinghouse for information and a unique if sometimes almost overwhelming learning experience.

For those for whom both the distance and expense of foreign travel, and the vast scale of the ICOC meetings, make a smaller, more focused, and more intimate conference more attractive, the recently instituted ACOR (American Conference on Oriental Rugs) provides an interesting alternative. Usually limited to a smaller number of participants—around 250—these annual mid-winter conferences usually involve a much more focused and limited schedule of presentations. Consequently, ACOR conferences pose fewer agonizing choices between events for those who attend.

LOOKING TO THE FUTURE

The recent formation of new rug societies in places as diverse as Atlanta and Detroit, the emergence of new periodic rug conferences under national sponsorship in Turkey and Iran, the continuing appearance of new and interesting publications on carpets, and the infusion of new material into the collector market as the result of political events in Eastern Europe and the republics of the former Soviet Union all point toward increasing opportunities for learning and collecting. The return to traditionally dyed carpets in Turkey and Iran, the emergence of new areas of collecting as new groups of old rugs are discovered, and the impact of contemporary Middle Eastern artists on carpet design suggest that the future of rug collecting will continue to be diverse and to expand its horizons. For those collectors with the right amounts of enthusiasm, patience, and knowledge, the fascinating world of the Oriental rug offers an ever-broadening series of new frontiers, in which history, culture, religion, and technique are combined in works of art that continue to intrigue and impress us by their combination of historical lineage and often mysterious beauty.

$\mathscr{W}$HERE TO SEE THE BEST EXAMPLES

IN NORTH AMERICA

Los Angeles   Los Angeles County Museum of Art: includes the less-well-known of the two Ardebil carpets in its collection. Carpets are rarely exhibited.

San Francisco   The Fine Arts Museums of San Francisco: Holdings include a large and important group of later carpets and kilims comprising the Caroline and H. McCoy Jones collection.

St. Louis   St. Louis Art Museum: Includes half of the celebrated collection of James Ballard. Carpets are occasionally exhibited.

Chicago   Chicago Art Institute: Many great classical carpets are held, but pieces are only rarely shown.

Kansas City   Nelson-Atkins Museum: Some important classical carpets are held, with a few examples on exhibition.

Oberlin, Ohio   The Allen Art Museum: A very good collection of more recent carpets, most from the Charles Martin Hall and Ernest Roberts collections. Some examples usually on display; occasional exhibitions.

Cincinnati The Markarian Foundation: Holds the collection of the late Richard Markarian, including some 160 carpets primarily of the later period of interest to collectors. No display facilities, but carpets are frequently loaned to exhibitions around the United States.

Washington, D.C. The Textile Museum: Has examples of great classical and more recent carpets in all categories. The museum's small galleries preclude large exhibitions, but parts of the collection are frequently displayed.

Philadelphia Philadelphia Museum of Art: This is one of the world's great collections of "showpiece" classical carpets. A few examples are usually on display.

New York Metropolitan Museum of Art: A great and comprehensive collection. There are examples from various Islamic countries on display in the museum's Islamic galleries.

Boston Musum of Fine Arts: A small but important collection of classical carpets and fragments. Holdings are very seldom displayed.

Cambridge, Massachusetts Harvard University Art Museums: A few classical pieces and a small but very fine collection of more recent rugs are exhibited from time to time in the Islamic gallery of the Arthur Sackler Museum.

Springfield, Massachusetts George Walter Vincent Smith Museum: One of America's great collections of more recent rugs, and of great interest to collectors. Some pieces are on exhibition in the Islamic gallery, and there are occasional larger exhibitions from the collection.

Richmond Virginia Museum of Fine Art: One of the most comprehensive collections of more recent carpets in the United States; some examples are rotated on exhibition in corridors.

Huntington, Virginia The Huntington Museum: A collection of rugs of interest to collectors, including around fifty rugs in the *sejjadeh* or prayer rug format.

Toronto, Canada Museum for Textiles: Canada's new museum devoted to textile arts. Has frequent exhibitions of carpets.

IN EUROPE

London Victoria and Albert Museum: A spectacular collection of early carpets, many on display in the museum's primary Islamic gallery and in corridors. Other examples are found in easy-access study storage.

Paris Museum of Decorative Arts: A fine collection of classical pieces, many on display in the Islamic galleries.

Lyons Museum of Historical Textiles: Another great French collection, with many examples on display in the Islamic galleries.

Berlin Berlin Museums: Since the reunification of the city and its museums, one of the most comprehensive of world carpet collections. Many examples are currently on display in the Islamic galleries in Dahlem (west Berlin) and the Islamic Museum in the Museum Island (east Berlin) branches of the reunited Berlin Museums.

Vienna Museum of Applied Arts: Probably the finest collection of great classical carpet showpieces in the world. Parts of the collection are often on display.

Budapest Museum of Applied Arts: A comprehensive collection of carpets, especially strong in Turkish examples from the seventeenth and eighteenth centuries. There are occasional exhibitions in the museum, and loan exhibitions to other Hungarian institutions.

Milan Poldi Pezzoli Museum: A few very important early carpets on permanent display.

Amsterdam Rijksmuseum: Some important classical carpets on display in the Islamic galleries.

Lisbon Calouste Gulbenkian Museum: A variety of early carpets on permanent display.

IN THE MIDDLE EAST

Istanbul Museum of Turkish and Islamic Art: One of the largest carpet collections in the world. Many of the most important examples of both recent and very old carpets are on display in the museum's large carpet galleries.

Istanbul Museum of Pious Foundations (Vakıflar Carpet Museum): Another spectacular collection, including Anatolian and other examples. The galleries for carpets show a small fraction of the collection. The kilim galleries are closed and the collection in storage under poor conditions, pending uncertain future developments.

Teheran Carpet Museum of Iran: Founded by the late shah, the status of the museum is uncertain. Recent visitors have been able to see the very rich collections, which consist almost entirely of Iranian carpets.

Kuwait City Kuwait National Museum: Islamic collections have been returned from Iraq, and the museum is under reconstruction. Includes a number of fine classical carpets.

Cairo Museum of Islamic Art: A number of examples of both recent and classical carpets are on permanent display.

CHAPTER 12

WHAT TO READ ABOUT ORIENTAL RUGS AND CARPETS

INTRODUCTORY BOOKS

Two introductory books are particularly useful. Jon Thompson's *Oriental Carpets* (New York: E. P. Dutton, 1988) is the best general introduction to carpets, with wonderful illustrations, and is still in print as of this writing. The older introduction by Walter Denny, *Oriental Rugs* (New York: Cooper-Hewitt Museum, 1979) is now out of print but is found in many libraries; it takes a more traditional approach.

RUG MANUALS

What we call "rug manuals" are books that attempt to be comprehensive guides for the collector. The most useful of these is

Murray Eiland's *Oriental Rugs: Expanded Edition* (Boston: New York Graphic Society, 1976), which is very broad in scope and covers the types of rugs from the four major traditional weaving areas that are most in demand by collectors. The illustrated examples are often not very exciting, but the book has a lot of very reliable information. More ambitious in scope, but perhaps of less practical use to the collector, is *World Rugs & Carpets,* edited by David Black (London: Country Life Books, 1985), with contributions by many authors. For coverage of rugs outside the four major weaving areas, Murray Eiland's *Chinese and Exotic Rugs* (Boston: New York Graphic Society, 1979) is still the most comprehensive book.

HISTORY OF CARPETS

Two old reliables are still among the major sources for carpet history, although they do not reflect recent discoveries. These are *Antique Rugs from the Near East,* Fourth Edition, by Wilhelm von Bode and Ernst Kuehnel, translated by Charles Grant Ellis (Ithaca, N.Y.: Cornell University Press, 1984), and Kurt Erdmann's *Oriental Carpets: An Account of Their History,* translated by Charles Grant Ellis (Fishguard, Wales: The Crosby Press, 1976), still a basic source for carpet history. The same author's *700 Years of Oriental Carpets* (Berkeley and Los Angeles: University of California Press, 1970) is a collection of short topical articles that together constitute a valuable background in carpet history for the collector. Basic information on the Pazyryk discoveries is contained in the archaeologist Sergei I. Rudenko's *Frozen Tombs of Siberia* (Berkeley and Los Angeles: University of California Press, 1970). Much of the nonsense written about the carpet since then is laid to rest in an article by H. Bohmer and J. Thompson, "The Pazyryk Carpet: A Technical Discussion," in *Source: Notes in the History of Art* (Vol. X, No. 4 [Summer, 1991], pp. 30–36). The history of carpets in general, and carpets in paintings in particular, are discussed in the magnificent and pivotal exhibition catalogue *The Eastern Carpet in the Western World* by Donald King and David Sylvester (London: Hayward Gallery/Arts Council of Great Britain, 1983). Onno Ydema's new book *Carpets and their Datings in Netherlandish Paintings 1540–1700* (Zutphen, Netherlands: Walburg Pers, 1991) is fascinating both as carpet history and in its application of computer analysis to carpet study.

BOOKS ON MAJOR GEOGRAPHIC AREAS

1. ANATOLIAN RUGS

Although collected for a long time, later Anatolian rugs have until quite recently not been the subject of much useful scholarship. The best general book, as much for its discussion of dyestuffs as for its catalogue, is *Rugs of the Peasants and Nomads of Anatolia,* by Werner Brüggemann and Harald Böhmer (Munich: Kunst und Antiquitäten Verlag, 1983), with 115 color plates. Recent nomadic rugs from Anatolia are discussed in Anthony Landreau and Ralph S. Yohe, *Flowers of the Yayla: Yörük Weaving of the Toros Mountains* (Washington, D.C.: The Textile Museum, 1983), another groundbreaking exhibition catalogue. Among the many recent books on Turkish flat weaves are Belkis Balpınar Acar's *Kilim—Cicim—Zili—Sumak: Turkish Flatweaves* (Istanbul: Eren Publishers, 1983), and the beautifully illustrated *Kilims: Masterpieces from Turkey* by Yanni Petsopoulos and Belkis Balpínar (New York: Rizzoli, 1991).

2. CAUCASIAN RUGS

Ulrich Schürmann's *Caucasian Rugs* (several editions and reprints available, published in both Germany and the United States), with its 160 color plates, is still the collector's bible of rug names from Transcaucasia. The catalogue by Charles Grant Ellis, *Early Caucasian Rugs* (Washington, D.C.: The Textile Museum, 1975) shows collectors the origins of their treasured designs. The "revisionist" writings of Richard Wright, including his catalogue *Rugs and Flatweaves of the Transcaucasus* (Pittsburgh: Pittsburgh Rug Society, 1980), are essential reading for the collector of "Caucasian" rugs.

3. IRANIAN RUGS

As a historical background to modern rugs of Iran, nothing can compare to the section on carpets in the venerable *Survey of Persian Art,* edited by Arthur Upham Pope and Phyllis Ackerman (various editions and reprints, Oxford University Press), including information on carpet structure and almost 170 illustrations. For the collector, the beautiful color plates in Erwin Gans-Ruedin's *The Splendor of Persian Carpets* (New York: Rizzoli, 1978) are a very useful introduction to types and designs. The collector will also find Michael Hillman's somewhat eccentric volume *Persian Carpets* (Austin: University of Texas Press, 1984) of some interest. The vast world of nomadic rugs from Iran has been covered in a number of very good recent books, among which James Opie's *Tribal Rugs of Southern Persia* (Portland, Ore.: James Opie Oriental Rugs, 1981) and Parviz Tanavoli's *Shahsavan: Iranian Rugs and Textiles* (New York: Rizzoli, 1985) may be noted for particularly useful illustrations and text.

4. TÜRKMEN RUGS

Ulrich Schürmann's *Central-Asian Rugs* (Frankfurt am Main: Österrieth, 1969) was the first "modern" general book to include the Türkmen, and two-thirds of the book's color plates are devoted to Türkmen examples. The most important book on Türkmen rugs to have appeared to date is the exhibition catalogue edited by Louise Mackie and Jon Thompson entitled *Türkmen: Tribal Carpets and Traditions* (Washington, D.C.: The Textile Museum, 1980). There are many, many other publications on Türkmen rugs, by authors such as Siawosch Azadi and Werner Loges, mostly published in Germany, that have splendid illustrations of splendid rugs.

5. OTHER RUGS

For Kurdish weaving, William Eagleton's *An Introduction to Kurdish Rugs* (New York: Interlink Books, 1988) and the catalogue edited by Robert Biggs entitled *Discoveries from Kurdish Looms* (Evanston, Ill.: Mary and Leigh Block Gallery, Northwestern University, 1983) are the basic works. For Moroccan rugs, another catalogue, edited by Patricia Fiske, W. R. Pickering, and Ralph Yohe, *From the Far West: Carpets and Textiles of Morocco* (Washington, D.C.: The Textile Museum, 1980), is the best introduction. Rugs with Armenian inscriptions are discussed in *Weavers, Merchants and Kings* (Fort Worth: Kimbell Art Museum, 1984) by Lucy der Manuelian and Murray Eiland. Rugs from India, both early and more recent, are lavishly illustrated in color in Erwin Gans-Ruedin's *Indian Carpets* (New York: Rizzoli, 1984).

BOOKS ON
TYPES AND
TECHNICAL CATEGORIES

Prayer rugs have been the subject of several books and exhibition catalogues; the most important and useful is by Richard Ettinghausen, Maurice Dimand, and Louise Mackie, entitled *Prayer Rugs* (Washington, D.C.: The Textile Museum, 1974).

Recently new books dealing with such categories of rugs as nomadic carpets, small bags, particular groups of designs, or particular techniques, have begun to appear in print. They tend for the most part to be either very broad or very narrow in scope, and some of them pursue rather eccentric theories. By contrast, two books dealing with flat-woven rugs—one by Anthony Landreau and W. R. Pickering, entitled *From the Bosphorus to Samarkand: Flat-Woven Rugs* (Washington, D.C.: The Textile Museum, 1969), and the kilim collector's bible, *Kilims* by Yanni Petsopoulos (New York: Rizzoli, 1979)—are useful basic works for the beginning collector.

BOOKS ON
MUSEUM COLLECTIONS

Because of the rising interest in books on carpets, many museums have recently found it economically feasible to publish catalogues of their carpet collections, and excellent volumes from institutions as diverse as the Berlin Museums and Colonial Williamsburg in Virginia have as a consequence appeared. Three museum catalogues are singled out here as having great educational benefit for the beginning collector, each in its own way. The very comprehensive collections of the Metropolitan Museum of Art were catalogued in Maurice Dimand and Jean Mailey, *Oriental Rugs in the Metropolitan Museum of Art* (New York: Metropolitan Museum of Art, 1973), a volume that serves as a general history of carpets as well as a collection catalogue. The two volumes by Belkis Balpınar and Udo Hirsch offering a selection of the most important pieces from Istanbul's extraordinarily rich Vakıflar Museum are entitled *Flatweaves of the Vakıflar Museum Istanbul* and *Carpets of the Vakıflar Museum Istanbul* (Wesel, Germany: Uta Hülsey, 1982 and 1988). Few books have done more to broaden our horizons of carpet-weaving than these two beautifully illustrated volumes. The grand old man of world carpet studies, Charles Grant Ellis, has published a catalogue entitled *Oriental Carpets in the Philadelphia Museum of Art* (Philadelphia: Philadelphia Museum of Art, 1988) that should serve into the foreseeable future as a model for the exhaustive scholarly study of older carpets. It is an instructive example of the merits of patience, thoroughness, and detail for the contemporary collector.

INFORMATION ON
TECHNIQUE AND
CARPET ANALYSIS

Most of the published material on carpet analysis and technique is included as an extra section in books dealing with other aspects of carpets. An exception is the booklet entitled *Notes on Carpet Weaving,* published in 1969 by the Victoria and Albert Museum in London. A recent essay on the subject intended for the layman and collector is "A Note on Technical and Structural Analysis" by Walter B. Denny, which appears in the catalogue of a large American private collection by W. Denny and D. Walker, *The Markarian Album* (Cincinnati: The Markarian Foundation, 1988, pp. 63–69).

INFORMATION ON
THE HISTORY OF
COLLECTING

The article by Russell S. Fling entitled "A History of Rug Collecting" in the Markarian volume cited immediately above is one informative and readable introduction to the history of rug collecting. Another is Julia W. Bailey's entertaining "Early Rug Collectors of New England" in Julia Bailey and Mark Hopkins, *Through the Collector's Eye: Oriental Rugs from New England Private Collections* (Providence: Museum of Art, Rhode Island School of Design, 1991). The Hajji Baba Club is discussed by Daniel Walker in *Oriental Rugs of the Hajji Babas* (New York: The Asia Society and Harry N. Abrams, 1982). Further information on European collecting history is found in Kurt Erdmann's *700 Years of Oriental Carpets* and the catalogue *The Eastern Carpet in the Western World* cited earlier in this chapter.

PRACTICAL CATEGORIES: CLEANING, REPAIR, DISPLAY

Until recently, reliable writing on these matters was difficult to find, and the most valuable information was hidden away in highly specialized publications dealing with museum conservation practice. The publication of Peter Stone's *Oriental Rug Repair* (Chicago: Greenleaf Company, 1981) has remedied this situation. The book, in addition to discussing rug repair in all of its aspects, covers cleaning, storage, and display of rugs.

MAGAZINES AND JOURNALS

Hali, the international journal of Oriental carpets and textiles, and *Oriental Rug Review (ORR)* have already been mentioned. Both contain information of great interest to collectors in their editorial pages, articles, and departments as well as in their advertisements. *Oriental Carpet and Textile Studies* is a journal that attempts to hold to high scholarly standards in its rug articles. Published in London on an irregular basis, it sometimes consists of the proceedings of rug conferences, which may be a very mixed *torba* indeed.

$\mathscr{G}$LOSSARY

Abrash Variations in color, generally seen in a pile rug as subtle horizontal bands, that are the indication of traditional dyeing practice. The wool is dyed in small lots resulting in minor variations in color (Plates 10, 14).

Adaptation The artistic process in which a weaver takes a design from another work of art, whether another rug, a textile, or a work in some other medium, and adapts the original to suit her own technique, the materials and colors available to her, and her own artistic preferences.

Aniline Early type of *industrial dye* (q.v.) invented in the mid-nineteenth century in Germany. Aniline-dyed wool is prone to fade or run when used in a rug. Common aniline dyes include fuchsine, a mauve that often fades to gray.

Bohcha Of Turkish origin, the word means "wrapper" and is used to describe a particular kind of bag made by folding four corners of a rug into a kind of envelope.

Boteh (also *buta, botta*) The Persian name for a characteristic "teardrop" motif that appears in Oriental carpets and textiles. Because it was the defining motif of copies of Indian wool shawls made in the Paisley mills in Scotland, it is commonly known as the Paisley motif.

Brocading The general term for various techniques used in *flat-woven* (q.v.) rugs of the sumak, zile, or jijim type, in which the design is formed by colorful supplementary wefts woven on top of the basic structure of warp and weft (Illus. 20).

C.E. Of the "common era"—a religiously and culturally neutral term now increasingly used for A.D. (*anno Domini*, "in the year of the Lord"). Since most countries of the world use the C.E. denomination today, and most are not of Christian heritage, use of the abbreviation is a considerate practice.

Chuval Of Turkish origin, the term may mean simply "sack." In Türkmen weaving, a chuval or juval is a large deep bag, wider than it is high, hung on the wall of a yurt dwelling (Plate 6).

DOBAG A Turkish acronym for Natural Dye Research and Development Project. Rugs woven in cooperatives organized by provincial govern-

191

ments in cooperation with Marmara University in Istanbul are allowed to carry the distinctive DOBAG label, which also includes the name of the weaver.

Elem   Türkmen term used for the skirts or flat-woven strips at the ends of carpets. It also applies to pile-woven end panels replacing the earlier flat-woven strips in some later Türkmen rugs.

Ensi (also *engsi;* sometimes also called *hachli,* meaning "with a cross")   In Türkmen weaving, a rug used as a doorway to the yurt or Turkmen nomadic dwelling (Illus. 21A).

Flat-woven (also *flat weave*)   Used to describe the technique of any carpet that does not use the knotted-pile technique, including, among others, the rugs known as *sumak, kilim,* and *jijim* (q.v.)

Gül (also *gul, göl;* in Persian, "flower")   In Türkmen weaving, used to describe the characteristic repetitive small medallion. It is thought to denote the tribal affiliation of the weaver.

Hali (also *khali, kali*)   Term of Turkish origin, used in the Middle East as the generic word for "rug"; also the name of the most important and comprehensive magazine devoted to carpets, published in London since 1978.

Handle   A term commonly used to characterize the weight, solidity, and flexibility of a rug. Adjectives used to describe handle include "stiff," "limp," and "flexible."

Heddle   A device on a loom that is composed of a stick or pole from which loops of cord capture those warps on the bottom side of the shed. Used to pull the "lower" warps through the "upper" warps on a loom in order to pass the weft through the space thereby created.

Hegira (from the Arabic *hijra,* meaning "escape, flight")   The Islamic system of reckoning historical dates, beginning on July 16, 622 C.E., uses a lunar year, which is a good deal shorter than a solar year. The calculation of equivalent dates thus involves a mathematical formula. Translation of dates are explained in G. S. P. Freeman-Grenville's book *The Muslim and Christian Calendars,* Second Edition (London: Rex Collings Ltd., 1977). The Hegira year 1415 began on June 10, 1994.

Heybe (also *khorjin*)   Usually refers to a characteristic double saddlebag woven in many parts of the Middle East (Plate 12).

Industrial dye (sometimes called "synthetic dye" or "chemical dye")   Dyestuff manufactured in chemical factories in Europe, or later in the Middle East. Includes *aniline dyes* (q.v.), azo dyes, and chrome dyes, all of which have been used for rug wool. Remember that *all* dyes are chemicals; few dyes are traditional.

mJijim (from the modern Turkish *cicim;* also *jajeem*)   Catchall term used to describe various *brocading* (q.v.) techniques in which the ornamental wefts do not completely cover the basic plain-weave structure. Also used to describe various genres of flat-woven rugs in Iran and Turkey.

Kejebe   Türkmen term used to describe a particular kind of large ceremonial animal trapping, sometimes with what appears to be a partial border around three sides (Illus. 21F).

Khorjin Common double saddlebag (see *Heybe*).

Kilim (also *gileem*) Flat-woven rug made in tapestry-weave technique, in which the colored wefts that form the pattern are beaten down to completely cover the warps. Includes the common slit-tapestry technique, where vertical slits separate areas of colored weft, and other techniques where slits are avoided by interlocking wefts with each other, or around a shared warp.

Knockout The private auction held by members of a dealer coalition to dispose of the rugs they have bought at public auction without bidding against each other. At the knockout, some dealers will get rugs while others will get money that otherwise would have gone to the original owner of the rug and the auctioneer.

Knot The basic unit of design and structure in a pile carpet, consisting of a piece of colored wool (or silk or cotton) yarn usually looped around two warps. It produces a colored tuft of wool on the front surface of the carpet (Illus. 17, 19).

Kpsi Knots per square inch. In the metric system, the common method of recording knot density is knots per square decimeter, or kpsd—i.e., knots in a square 10 centimeters on a side, containing a hundred square centimeters. To get approximate kpsd, simply multiply kpsi by 15.5.

Mafrash A term of Turkish origin, it refers to a medium-sized horizontal bag woven by nomadic peoples in various parts of the rug-weaving world (Illus. 21C).

Mihrab Arabic word for niche in a mosque or community prayer hall indicating the direction of Mecca toward which Muslims face when they pray. It is also a term sometimes applied to the pointed archlike form in a *sejjadeh* (q.v.), or prayer rug.

Mosque (from the Arabic *masjid*—literally, "place of prostration") In the Islamic world, a building for community prayer whose floors are often covered with carpets.

Namazlyk A term combining Persian and Turkish words—literally, "for prayer" (see *Sejjadeh*).

ORR *Oriental Rug Review,* a magazine published in New Hampshire, and an often irreverent challenger to the more sophisticated *Hali.*

Roller beam A type of vertical loom in which warps are unrolled from a rotatable horizontal, cylindrical beam at the top of the loom as the finished rug is rolled up on a similar cylinder at the bottom. It allows for the weaving of a long rug on a short loom (Illus. 12).

Saff (Arabic—literally, "rank" or "row") Applied to large carpets designed for use in mosques, with designs divided into rows of compartments, each suitable as a place for one individual to pray.

Sejjadeh (Arabic—literally, "for prostration," and prayer rug, *namazlyk.*) The generic term for a rug about 3½ by 5½ feet suitable for one individual to use for prayer. Also applied to rugs of this size with a design of a symbolic arch, doorway, or *mihrab* (q.v.) indicating the direction of prayer or the gateway to heaven (Plates 2–6).

Selvedge   The characteristic side finish of a rug, generally consisting of one or more warps wrapped with wefts or with added colored wool yarns.

Shed stick   The stick used on the loom to separate the warps alternately into two levels. It is usually a broad flat stick of wood (Illus. 13).

Shill   Individual, usually in the employ of an unscrupulous auctioneer, who makes false bids at an auction with the intent of artificially driving up the price of a rug.

Skirt   See *Elem.*

Slit tapestry   See *Kilim.*

Stylization   The artistic process whereby an element of carpet design gradually changes over time as the result of repeated *adaptations* (q.v.) by individual weavers from their models. This usually results in gradual simplification of original forms, together with a movement away from curvilinear forms toward geometric forms.

Sumak   A particular kind of brocading in which the supplementary wefts are passed over and then back under the warps according to a particular formula (Illus. 20).

Talim   (Arabic—literally, "instruction")   Term used in Iran for a document written in special notation that can be read aloud as a set of knotting instructions to weavers sitting at the loom.

Torba   (Turkish word)   A small bag, in Türkmen weaving much wider than deep, used for small items of clothing or utensils in the nomadic tent or yurt.

Traditional dyes   (sometimes called "natural dyes" or "vegetable dyes")   Dyes made and used in traditional rug-weaving societies in the historic past, usually derived from plant materials such as indigo or madder root, but also made from amalgams of materials such as walnut husks and iron filings.

Vagireh   (Persian word, also spelled *wagireh*) Sometimes called a "sampler," a type of small commercial rug usually woven in Iran in which a variety of border and field ornaments are often arbitrarily woven as a sampling of ornaments available in larger carpets.

Warp   The lengthwise or vertical structural elements attached to the two end beams of a loom upon which a rug is woven by the addition of weft and pile (Illus. 10).

Weft   (also *woof*) The widthwise or horizontal structural elements of a rug, passed over and under the warps by manipulation of the *heddle* and the *shed stick* (q.v.), that form part of the basic structure or foundation of a pile rug, and that form the design of flat-woven rugs.

Yastık   (Turkish term meaning "cushion") A small rug, usually woven with a knotted pile, about 3 feet long by 16 inches wide (Plate 15).

INDEX

Note: Italicized page numbers refer to illustration captions.

ABOUT THE AUTHOR

Walter B. Denny is professor of art history at the University of Massachusetts, Amherst, and honorary curator of carpets and textiles at the Harvard University Art Museums. In addition to having served as a trustee of The Textile Museum in Washington, D.C., he is consultant and adviser to many institutions in the United States and abroad. He is the author of *Oriental Rugs*, published by the Cooper-Hewitt Museum of the Smithsonian Institution, and is an editor of *Oriental Carpet and Textile Studies*.